THE HR CLIMATE OF THE WORLD

Embracing Cultural Diversity

SUNIIL PATHARE

This is a work of nonfiction. The events and the incidents mentioned in the book are true and real. Howerever, some names and characteristics have been changed, some events have been compressed, and some dialogues have been recreated.

First Edition: February 2025
Printed in India

Printed at: Padmavati Art Print, Mumbai
Typeset in Times New Roman

ISBN: 978-93-6070-004-1

Cover Design: Prajakta Sawant

STORYMIRROR
Stories that reflect you

Publisher: StoryMirror Infotech Pvt. Ltd.
Unit No-F/705, 7th Floor, Kailas Corporate Lounge,
Veer Savarkar Road, Vikhroli Park Site,
Vikhroli West, Mumbai-400079,
Maharashtra, India.

Web: storymirror.com
Facebook: @storymirror
Twitter: @story_mirror
Instagram: @storymirror
Email: marketing@storymirror.com

Words of Praise

"The HR Climate of the World" is an extraordinary exploration of how people shape organizations and how culture, technology, and humanity must coexist for sustainable success. The book captures the evolving dimensions of HR with depth and authenticity, making it both a practical guide and a thought-provoking read. In an era defined by stress, mental health challenges, and rapid technological change, this work reminds us that great organizations are ultimately built by great human beings. Kudos to Suniil Pathare for creating one of the most insightful contributions to modern HR thinking.

Sunil Chari
Managing Director,
Rossari Biotech Ltd.

"Suniil Pathare's *The HR Climate of the World* takes us on an insightful journey through the changing landscape of workplace culture. It highlights how human connection and understanding remain the foundation of successful organizations, irrespective of geography or generation. A timely and valuable contribution to modern HR thinking."

Robin Banerjee
Author & Chairman, Nucleon Research Pvt. Ltd.

"*The HR Climate of the World* is an insightful and thought-provoking read that brings rare clarity to one of the most complex subjects in modern business — managing people across cultures.

As an entrepreneur and author, I found the book to be a masterclass in understanding global workforce behaviour and cultural intelligence that truly bridges people, purpose, and progress." It beautifully connects real-world HR practices with human values, making it not just informative but deeply relevant for every business leader navigating today's interconnected world."

Kapil Pathare
Author & Deputy Managing Director
- VIP Clothing Ltd.

Suniil Pathare brings rare depth to the subject of human resources, shaped by several decades of leading VIP Clothing Ltd. and engaging with diverse business cultures across the world. His deep observations on how HR has evolved with changing times make this book both insightful and highly relevant. *The HR Climate of the World* is a remarkable contribution — a collector's edition that will guide business students, HR professionals, and corporate leaders in building future-ready, people-centric organizations.

Meher Castelino
Fashion & Corporate Communication Consultant,
Author & Femina Miss India 1964

"Being a surgeon, far away from the boardroom, I did not expect to connect with this book — but I was pleasantly surprised. The lessons shared are relevant not only to corporations but even in hospitals and clinics. The book beautifully explains how cultural and geographic differences shape people's approach to work, and how good leadership can bring them together towards a shared purpose. What I found most valuable is its focus on humanity in HR — creating an environment where every individual feels safe, involved, and growing. This is a must-read that transcends industries and inspires thoughtful leadership. I strongly recommend it to all professionals and anyone in a responsible role."

Dr. Rajendra Sonavane
Consultant General & GI Surgeon

"The HR Climate of the World" is an exceptional global study of people, culture and leadership across continents. The book highlights how human behaviour, workplace expectations and habits differ from country to country — supported by rich case studies and practical examples. It skillfully connects cultural realities with HR strategy, helping readers understand what truly drives performance in diverse environments. Suniil Pathare has created a valuable resource for industry leaders seeking to build organizations that thrive in a multicultural world.

Chandrakant Salunkhe
Founder & President,
SME Chamber of India

“The HR Climate of the World” by Shri Suniil Pathare is a remarkable synthesis of research, insight, and real-world experience that redefines the global HR narrative. It bridges cultures, connects theory with practice, and highlights how sustainability, collaboration, and social responsibility can transform organizations. With clarity and vision, the book offers a roadmap for leaders and HR professionals to shape an inclusive, high-performing, and future-ready workforce. A truly outstanding contribution to the evolving world of human resource management, it inspires a new way of thinking about people, culture, and purpose in business.

Dr. Naresh Chandra
Director (Education), B. K. Birla College, Kalyan
Former Pro-Vice Chancellor, University of Mumbai

EPIGRAPH

"Embracing cultural diversity in the workplace is not just a responsibility, but an opportunity—an opportunity to unlock the full potential of a global workforce and build stronger, more inclusive organizations."

The HR Climate of the World
— Embracing Cultural Diversity

Acknowledgement

Writing this book has been an incredible journey, and I owe its completion to the unwavering support and inspiration of those around me. I would like to extend my deepest gratitude to my family and friends, who have been my pillars of strength throughout this process. A special thanks to Kapil Pathare, Robin Banerjee, Gopal Sehjpal, Monica Schmitt, Dr. Rajendra Sonavane, Dr. Yogesh Palshetkar, Dr. Nanjappa Kandarthanda, Dr. Sandeep Jadhav, Dr. Prashant Sonavane, Johar Zojwalla, Sunil Chari, Jatin Sablok, Vikas Pathare, Hemant Chemburkar, Suresh Bhatia, Jitendra Cheema, Ashish Shete, Vandana Shete, Sanjay Pathare, Vijay Churi, Nitin Churi, Vikas Bhatnagar, Dinesh Kedia, Avinash Bhatnagar, Dr. Anay Aher, Dr. Abhijit Wadekar, Ashok Bhatia, Shriram Chari, Chandrakant Salunke, Dilip Bhatt, Rohan Bhargava, Dr. Naresh Chandra, Late Shri Dr. Arvind Kulkarni, Late Shri Ashok Pradhan, Manohar Palan, and Kanishk Pathare. Our countless discussions—sometimes knowingly and many times unknowingly—on the themes and topics covered in this book have played a crucial role in shaping the ideas within these pages.

I would also like to acknowledge Kristina David, a former cross-border employee from Hungary who worked with my organization in India for five years. Her insights into bridging cultures were instrumental in helping me appreciate the rich and diverse perspectives across borders.

My global travels further deepened this understanding, offering me a firsthand view of how different cultures interact and blend in the professional world. A heartfelt thanks to my Executive Assistant, Rupal Shedge, the VIP Clothing Company, Board members and the HR team, whose valuable input helped guide the selection of topics and content for this book.

I am also deeply grateful to my overseas friends and family — Ajay Singh from Germany, Nayan Shrivastava from Switzerland, Yogesh Patel from the USA, Ronak Upadhyay from the UK, Manohar Hemrajani from the UAE, Tanushree Joshi from Maldives, A.S Lal from UAE, Monica Smith from Germany, Harish Giri from Germany, Ujjwala Raut from the USA, Abby Lau from Singapore, Dirk Bachmann from Germany, Soni Jagwani from Japan, Vikram Shetty from Zambia, Sethu Bhattacharya from Saudi Arabia & UAE, Missy Amran from Indonesia, Jean Bhatia from USA, Dominique Seau from France, Viren Dugal from Indonesia, Viren Pathare from USA, Mahesh Modi from Saudi Arabia & Qatar, Kaizar Lashkari from Singapore, Hanane Fessikh from Morocco and Italy, William Harp from Hong Kong and China, Stephanie Cafiero from Italy & Brazil, N.S Kumar from Belgium, Vaishali Doshi from Australia, Manju Hirani & Navin Daryani from Canada, Yulai Kuzmenko from Ukraine, Smita Mahimkar from New Zealand, Rohit Tamane from Canada, Jelena Matvejevskaja from Estonia, Akshay Dixit from the Czech Republic, Julia Ivanova from Russia,Marco Areias from Portugal, Ojy Okpe from USA & Nigeria, Rotash Tulyani from Kenya, and Saidah Jules from Russia. Their insights into their respective cultures have been invaluable. I also want to express my gratitude to my friends from the Lions community—Pankaj Mehta, Dwarka Jalan, Surendra Sharma, B.R. Mehta, Rajesh Mehra, Anand Mehta and Ruchita Mehra—whose perspectives have also contributed to this work.

Finally, I dedicate this book to my two gurus—my father, the late Shri Jaykumar Pathare, and his partner and friend, Late Shri L. Jaipal Reddy—who have been the true sources of my inspiration and direction, providing me with the life lessons and wisdom that I carry with me today. I also express my heartfelt gratitude to my mother - Smt. Lalita Pathare, my wife - Heena Pathare, my sister-in-law - Ashwini Pathare, and my niece - Avyukta Pathare, for being unwavering companions in this journey—understanding me, supporting me throughout, and most importantly, helping me appreciate the differences in motherhood and childhood experiences across the world. Their insights and strength have been vital to this book's emotional and cultural depth.

Preface

As the world becomes increasingly interconnected, the role of Human Resources has evolved into something far more complex, dynamic, and impactful. This book, *The HR Climate of the World: Embracing Cultural Diversity,* is born out of a vision to explore how organizations can successfully navigate the multifaceted cultural landscapes that shape today's global workforce.

At the heart of this book lies the conviction that cultural diversity, once seen as a challenge, is now an invaluable strategic and synergistic asset. By embracing this diversity, organizations can foster innovation, strengthen team cohesion, and unlock unprecedented potential within their workforce. This book offers a comprehensive lens into the practices, trends, and strategies employed by leading organizations worldwide to create inclusive environments where employees from diverse backgrounds can thrive together.

Through the chapters that follow, I delve into the intricate nuances of cultural diversity and how they shape workforce behavior. For instance, the cultural roots of tardiness often reflect deeply ingrained childhood habits, influenced by societal norms in different parts of the world. In some cultures, punctuality is rigorously instilled from an early age, while in others, a more relaxed approach to time reflects community values or flexible perceptions of schedules. Understanding these variations is essential for HR professionals to address workplace expectations effectively and empathetically.

This book provides actionable insights for HR professionals to develop policies and strategies that support a truly global workforce. Drawing on real-world examples, interviews with industry leaders, and cutting-edge research, this work is designed to be both a practical guide and a source of inspiration for leaders and HR practitioners. The goal is to empower organizations to foster unity in diversity and cultivate workplaces where everyone feels respected, valued, and empowered to contribute their best.

The HR Climate of the World: Embracing Cultural Diversity seeks to highlight the immense potential of cultural diversity and the pivotal role HR plays in unleashing it. By embracing the principles outlined in this book, organizations can build resilient, inclusive, and culturally enriched teams that thrive in today's interconnected world.

It is my hope that this book not only serves as a roadmap for HR professionals but also inspires a broader conversation about the transformative power of cultural diversity in the workplace. Together, let us embark on this journey to discover and celebrate the vast human potential within our globally diverse world.

Suniil Pathare
Author

Introduction:
The Global HR Landscape

In an era where borders are increasingly porous and technology has made the world smaller than ever, the realm of Human Resources (HR) finds itself at a fascinating crossroads. Gone are the days when HR practices were siloed within national boundaries, adhering strictly to local customs and regulations. Today, we stand on the precipice of a truly global workforce, one that demands a reimagining of how we approach talent management, employee engagement, and organizational culture.

"The HR Climate of the World" is not just a book; it's a journey across continents, cultures, and corporations. It's an exploration of how the human element of business is evolving in response to global forces, technological advancements, and shifting societal expectations. As we traverse this landscape, we'll uncover the challenges and opportunities that arise when managing people becomes a global endeavor.

Consider for a moment the complexity of today's multinational corporations. A team meeting might include participants from Tokyo, Toronto, and Tunis, each bringing their own cultural perspectives and working within their local labour laws. The HR professional tasked with fostering collaboration, ensuring compliance, and driving performance in such an environment faces a multifaceted challenge that would have been almost unimaginable just a few decades ago.

But it's not just the multinational giants that are affected by the globalizing HR climate. Small businesses, too, find themselves competing for talent on an international stage, leveraging remote work to tap into a worldwide talent pool. Start-ups in Bengaluru vie for software engineers alongside tech giants in Silicon Valley. A graphic designer in Barcelona might work for clients in New York, Sydney, and Cape Town—all without leaving his or her home office.

Throughout this book, we'll delve into the myriad factors shaping the global HR landscape:

- How do cultural differences impact management styles and employee expectations across regions?
- What role does technology play in bridging geographical divides and creating new paradigms for work, Leadership challenges and management styles?
- How are companies navigating the complex web of international labour laws and regulations?
- What strategies are proving effective in fostering diversity, equity, and inclusion on a global scale?

- How are compensation and benefits evolving to meet the needs of a global workforce?
- What does the future hold for HR as we continue to push the boundaries of how and where work is done?

By examining case studies, analysing trends, and drawing insights from HR leaders around the world, we'll paint a comprehensive picture of the current state of global HR and peek into its future. Whether you're an HR professional looking to expand your international expertise, a business leader aiming to build a more globally competitive organization, or simply someone fascinated by the changing nature of work in our interconnected world, this book offers valuable insights and practical strategies.

As we embark on this exploration of the world's HR climate, we invite you to leave behind preconceived notions, outdated management philosophies and practices (e.g. performance management practices and promotion from within policies, etc.) and embrace the complexity and richness of our global business ecosystem. The challenges are significant, but so too are the opportunities for those who can navigate this new landscape with new skills, insights and foresight.

Welcome to "The HR Climate of the World"—let's begin our journey.

Table of Contents

Part I: Cultural and Regional Foundations

Part II: Technological Evolution and Workforce Innovation

PART I:

Cultural and Regional Foundations

"Tardiness is more than a momentary delay—it's a reflection of deeply ingrained cultural habits. To understand workforce behavior, we must first understand the rhythms of time that each culture follows."

Chapter 1

The Cultural Roots of Tardiness:

Unveiling the Behavioural Habits Shaping the Global Workforces

In the global landscape of contemporary business, the role of Human Resources (HR) transcends traditional boundaries, adapting to the diverse cultural and societal norms of different continents. HR professionals face unique challenges that are deeply influenced by regional behaviours, historical contexts, and cultural attitudes. Among these challenges, managing employee punctuality is a universal concern that manifests differently across various parts of the world. This chapter examines how HR strategies for addressing punctuality reveal the distinct human behaviours and cultural nuances of different regions.

Asia and India: The Cultural Roots of Tardiness

One of the most significant cultural traits influencing workplace behaviour in Asia, particularly in India, is tardiness. While tardiness may appear as a superficial issue, it is deeply rooted in the social and familial structures that shape individuals from their earliest years. This chapter examines how these cultural underpinnings, particularly those related to family and school dynamics in India, manifest in the workplace. By understanding the cultural origins of tardiness, HR professionals can better address punctuality and productivity challenges in these regions.

Tardiness in India, and much of Asia, is not merely a reflection of individual habits; it is intricately linked to cultural norms that begin forming in childhood. In India, parents often take an active role in managing their children's daily routines—whether it is waking them up for school, ensuring they have breakfast, or packing their school bags. Children grow up with a dependency on this external structure, where they are not always responsible for their own punctuality.

Parents push their children to rise on time, get ready for school, and adhere to a strict routine, yet much of this effort is managed by the parents rather than the children themselves. This creates a dependency that spills over into adulthood, where individuals lack the intrinsic motivation to be punctual or take responsibility for their own time management.

Example: The Morning Rush Phenomenon

In many Indian households, the morning routine is a family affair. Parents, especially mothers, take on the task of getting children ready for school, which often involves multiple rounds of wake-up calls, preparing meals, and ensuring children leave the house on time. This external imposition of time management does not allow children to develop their sense of urgency or responsibility toward punctuality.

By the time these children enter the workforce, the habit of waiting for external prompts to act often remains ingrained. They may rely on reminders from managers or colleagues to complete tasks or meet deadlines, leading to issues with tardiness and time management in professional settings.

The Role of Schooling in Shaping Time Discipline

The Indian education system, with its rigid structure and time-bound schedules, paradoxically contributes to the issue of tardiness. While schools impose strict timelines—such as arrival times, class periods, and exam schedules—the enforcement of these rules often relies on external punishment rather than internal motivation. Students may adhere to school schedules to avoid reprimands and lose grades, but this external discipline doesn't instil a personal commitment to punctuality.

As these students transition into the workforce, they often struggle with time discipline unless they are in environments with strong oversight, supervision and micro-management. This cultural root of tardiness, stemming from childhood dependence on external control, is a challenge HR professionals (or the immediate supervisor/manager/boss) must navigate when managing time-sensitive tasks and workplace punctuality.

Case Study: Addressing Tardiness in an Indian IT Firm

An Indian IT company faced significant delays in project timelines due to the habitual tardiness of its employees. Rather than focusing solely on punitive measures, the HR team introduced a new program designed to cultivate time management, discipline, behaviour and attitude among employees. Workshops on personal responsibility, along with mentorship programs encouraging senior employees to model punctuality, helped address the cultural root of the problem.

By acknowledging that tardiness was not merely a behavioural issue but one deeply embedded in the cultural upbringing of the employees, the HR team was able to approach the problem with empathy and design solutions that fostered personal growth and accountability.

The Broader Asian Context: Cultural Roots of Tardiness

While India provides a clear example, other Asian countries share similar cultural traits influencing punctuality. In countries like Thailand, Indonesia, and the Philippines, community living and family-centered values often take precedence over rigid adherence to time schedules. The concept of "rubber time" is prevalent in many Southeast Asian cultures, where timelines are viewed more flexibly, and arriving late is not necessarily seen as disrespectful.

This cultural tendency is rooted in the prioritization of relationships over tasks. In many Asian societies, maintaining harmony in relationships is considered more important than strict adherence to punctuality. Consequently, in professional settings, employees may prioritize finishing a conversation with a colleague or addressing a family matter over arriving on time for a meeting.

In Asia, and particularly in India, punctuality issues are a prevalent concern for HR departments. Employees frequently arrive late, prompting HR to enforce stringent policies on attendance, including deductions in leave or pay. This habitual tardiness can often be traced back to childhood routines. In India, for example, parents rushing their children to school is still a pattern of last-minute urgency that persists into adulthood and professional life. This ingrained habit presents a significant challenge for HR, which must balance the enforcement of punctuality with an understanding of these deeply rooted cultural behaviors.

Infosys, a global leader in technology services and consulting, faced challenges with punctuality among its Indian workforce. By introducing flexible work hours and implementing a comprehensive time management training program, Infosys was able to improve punctuality without sacrificing employee satisfaction. The company reported a 15% increase in overall productivity within the first year of these changes.

Tata Consultancy Services (TCS) has implemented a policy known as "Flexi-Time" to address the cultural issues related to tardiness. This policy allows employees to have a flexible start time, provided they complete the required number of hours each day. This approach respects the cultural context of tardiness while ensuring that work is completed efficiently.

Geert Hofstede's Cultural Dimensions Theory provides a framework for understanding how cultural differences impact workplace behavior. In high-context cultures like India, where personal relationships and social hierarchies are paramount, flexibility in time management is often necessary to accommodate social obligations and familial responsibilities. HR practices must therefore be adapted to respect these cultural dimensions, thereby fostering an environment where employees can effectively balance their professional and personal commitments.

Middle East and Gulf: Balancing Flexibility and Authority

In the Middle East and Gulf regions, the workforce often displays a more relaxed attitude toward punctuality, coupled with a strong sense of individualism and authority. Employees in these regions may exhibit a preference for operating on their own schedules, reflecting broader cultural norms that prioritize personal autonomy and status. For HR professionals, this necessitates a delicate balance between enforcing punctuality and respecting cultural attitudes.

In Dubai's free zones, businesses operate with a high degree of flexibility, attracting international talent and investment. Companies in these areas often allow flexible working hours to accommodate diverse cultural practices and improve employee morale. This approach has helped Dubai maintain its status as a leading business hub in the Middle East.

"In the Middle East, the concept of time is often more fluid, and HR strategies must be adaptable to respect these cultural nuances while ensuring productivity." - Dr. Mohamed Ramady, Economic Advisor and Author

Edward T. Hall's theory on high-context and low-context cultures provides insight into why flexibility is crucial in the Middle East. High-context cultures rely on implicit communication and the context surrounding interactions.

In such environments, rigid time structures may be seen as less important than maintaining social harmony and respecting hierarchical relationships. HR policies that offer flexibility and emphasize relational management are more likely to succeed.

Europe: Productivity Over Presence

European countries generally prioritize productivity and quality of work over strict adherence to time spent in the office. From an early age, Europeans are taught the values of self-discipline, precision, and a focus on outcomes. This cultural emphasis on efficiency and effectiveness influences HR policies, which often show leniency towards exact start times as long as work objectives are achieved.

European countries exhibit a high level of precision and attention to detail in the workplace. This emphasis on precision is not an accident—it is deeply ingrained in the education system and social structures from early childhood. In many parts of Europe, children are taught from a young age to approach tasks with a focus on exactness, accuracy, and discipline.

Example: Childhood Learning and Precision in Schools

One telling example comes from childhood education in countries like Germany and Switzerland, where even seemingly simple tasks such as folding paper or making the four corners of a piece of paper meet perfectly are part of school exercises. Teachers emphasize the importance of neatness and accuracy, instilling in students a mindset that attention to small details is crucial.

This cultural emphasis on precision extends to the workplace, where European employees often demonstrate strong organizational skills, a focus on process adherence, and a commitment to high-quality outputs. In manufacturing, engineering, and even administrative roles, precision is regarded as a vital value that drives efficiency and productivity.

Small Details, Big Impact.

Case Study: German Engineering

The German engineering sector is often heralded for its precision and quality. Much of this reputation can be traced back to the cultural emphasis on meticulousness that begins in childhood. In Germany, the term "Ordnung" (order) reflects the deep-seated belief that precision and orderliness lead to success. This cultural trait is evident in how employees approach tasks, whether it's designing complex machinery or executing a production schedule down to the minute.

Siemens, a multinational conglomerate headquartered in Germany, has implemented a flexible working hours policy known as the "New Way of Working" initiative. This policy allows employees to choose their working hours as long as they meet their performance targets. The initiative has led to increased job satisfaction and a 20% improvement in productivity.

In Scandinavian countries such as Sweden and Denmark, there is a strong emphasis on achieving a work-life balance and maintaining productivity. Companies often implement policies that allow for flexible working hours and remote work options. This approach not only enhances productivity but also ensures high levels of employee well-being and satisfaction.

Max Weber's concept of the Protestant Work Ethic, which emphasizes hard work, discipline, and efficiency, is deeply embedded in many European cultures. This work ethic supports a results-oriented approach, where the quality and efficiency of work are valued over the mere presence of employees in the office. HR strategies that align with these cultural values by promoting productivity and providing flexibility tend to be more effective.

United States: Innovation and Flexibility

In the United States, the stereotype of employees being lazy or careless is a simplification that overlooks the complex and dynamic nature of the American work culture. While Americans may approach work with a degree of casualness, HR strategies focus on creating motivational and engaging work environments. The US work culture is characterized by its emphasis on innovation, creativity, and flexibility, often at the expense of rigid punctuality. HR practices in the US include performance-based incentives, flexible scheduling, and a strong focus on employee engagement and satisfaction, aims to harness the creative potential of the workforce while maintaining accountability.

Google's HR practices are a prime example of balancing flexibility and innovation. By offering flexible work hours, remote work options, and a vibrant workplace culture, Google fosters an environment of creativity and high performance. The company's approach to HR has been instrumental in driving innovation and maintaining its position as a leader in the tech industry.

Netflix has a unique approach to HR, characterized by its "Freedom and Responsibility" culture. Employees are given the freedom to manage their own schedules and are evaluated based on their contributions and results rather than the hours they clock. This culture of trust and accountability has been key to Netflix's innovation and success.

Abraham Maslow's Hierarchy of Needs theory can be applied to understand American work culture. By focusing on higher-level needs such as self-actualization and esteem, American HR practices aim to create work environments that foster innovation, creativity, and personal growth. Flexible scheduling and performance-based rewards align with the goal of fulfilling employees' higher-order needs, thereby driving engagement and productivity.

Far East: Discipline and Precision

Countries in the Far East, such as Japan and South Korea, are renowned for their punctuality and disciplined work ethic. Employees in these regions are expected to adhere strictly to schedules, with the workday meticulously structured to maximize efficiency. This cultural norm of timeliness and respect for deadlines is deeply ingrained, making the role of HR in enforcing punctuality relatively straightforward.

Toyota's success is often attributed to its disciplined approach to work and adherence to the principles of the Toyota Production System (TPS). The company's HR practices emphasize punctuality, continuous improvement (Kaizen), and respect for individuals, resulting in a highly efficient and productive workforce.

"In Japan, punctuality is a reflection of respect and dedication. It's deeply embedded in our work culture and essential for maintaining harmony and efficiency." - Akio Toyoda, President of Toyota Motor Corporation

The Confucian work ethic, which emphasizes discipline, respect for hierarchy, and collective harmony, is deeply ingrained in the cultures of Japan, South Korea, and other

Far Eastern countries. This cultural framework supports a disciplined approach to work, where punctuality and adherence to schedules are seen as expressions of respect and responsibility. HR practices that align with these values by enforcing strict attendance policies and promoting continuous improvement are more effective in these contexts.

Africa: Flexibility and Adaptability

In Africa, the approach to work and punctuality can vary widely across the continent, reflecting its rich diversity of cultures and societal norms. Generally, there is a more relaxed attitude towards time, with employees often working at their own pace. This requires HR professionals to adopt flexible management styles that are sensitive to local cultural contexts.

Safaricom, a leading telecommunications company in Kenya, has successfully navigated the challenges of managing a diverse workforce by implementing flexible work arrangements and performance-based metrics. This approach has allowed Safaricom to maintain high levels of employee engagement and productivity while respecting cultural differences.

MTN Group, a multinational telecommunications company operating across Africa, has adopted flexible working hours and telecommuting policies to accommodate the diverse cultural attitudes towards time. This flexibility has enabled MTN to attract and retain talent across various regions, contributing to its growth and success.

Anthropologist Edward T. Hall's distinction between polychronic and monochronic time systems helps explain the varied approaches to time in Africa. Polychronic cultures, which are prevalent in many parts of Africa, view time as fluid and multitasking as natural. HR strategies that recognize and adapt to these cultural preferences by allowing for flexible schedules and task-oriented goals are more likely to succeed in such environments. In contrast, monochronic cultures, which are common in Western societies, view time as linear, compartmentalized, and task-focused. These cultures emphasize punctuality, planning, and adherence to schedules. Individuals are generally expected to complete one task at a time and prioritize deadlines over spontaneous social interaction. Time is often treated as a resource—something that can be saved, lost, spent, or wasted.

Australia: Work-Life Balance

Australia is renowned for its laid-back lifestyle, which is also reflected in its work culture. While punctuality is valued, there is also a strong emphasis on work-life balance. HR practices in Australia often focus on creating a harmonious work environment where employees feel valued and motivated. This emphasis on balance ensures high productivity without compromising personal well-being.

Atlassian, an Australian enterprise software company, exemplifies the country's commitment to work-life balance. Atlassian offers flexible working hours and remote work options, which allow employees to balance their professional responsibilities with personal commitments. The company also promotes mental health initiatives, such as providing access to counselling services and mental health days. These practices have resulted in high employee satisfaction and retention rates, contributing to Atlassian's reputation as a top employer.

The Commonwealth Bank of Australia (CBA) has implemented a range of flexible working arrangements to support work-life balance. Employees can choose from flexible start and finish times, part-time work arrangements, and job-sharing options. The Bank also offers generous parental leave and return-to-work programs to support employees with families. These initiatives help CBA attract and retain a diverse and talented workforce.

Work-life balance theory emphasizes the importance of achieving a balance between professional and personal life to enhance overall well-being and productivity. In Australia, HR practices that prioritize work-life balance align with this theory by offering flexible work arrangements, supportive policies for parents, and initiatives to promote mental and physical health. These practices not only improve employee satisfaction but also boost organizational performance.

South America: Community and Collaboration

In South America, the workplace is often characterized by a strong sense of community and collaboration. Employees value personal relationships and teamwork, which influences their approach to work and punctuality.

HR professionals in South America focus on creating a supportive and inclusive work environment that fosters collaboration and mutual respect.

Natura & Co, a Brazilian multinational cosmetics company, emphasizes community and collaboration in its HR practices. The company promotes open communication, teamwork, and social responsibility, creating a culture where employees feel connected and motivated. Natura's inclusive work environment has been instrumental in its growth and success.

Grupo Bimbo, a Mexican multinational bakery product manufacturing company, fosters a collaborative work culture through team-building activities, employee engagement programs, and a focus on corporate social responsibility. These practices help build a sense of community and loyalty among employees, enhancing productivity and job satisfaction.

Social capital theory highlights the importance of networks, relationships, and social interactions in achieving organizational goals. In South America, HR practices that build social capital by fostering collaboration, trust, and mutual support are effective in creating a cohesive and productive work environment. These practices leverage the strong community-oriented culture to drive organizational success.

Navigating Cultural Differences in HR

HR practices around the world are deeply influenced by a complex interplay of cultural, social, and historical factors. Understanding these differences is crucial for HR professionals working in multinational organizations or those aiming to implement best practices across diverse regions. By appreciating the unique contexts of each continent, HR can develop more effective and culturally appropriate strategies to manage workforce behavior, enhance organizational performance, and create a harmonious global workplace.

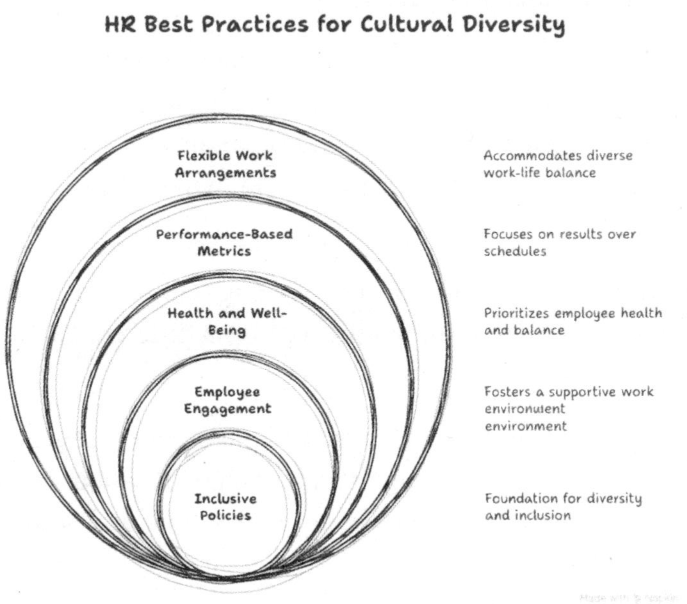

Global Perspective: Best Practices

While regional differences necessitate tailored HR strategies, certain best practices can be applied universally to navigate cultural differences effectively:

1. Cultural Sensitivity Training: Provide training to HR professionals and managers on cultural differences and their impact on workplace behavior. This training helps build awareness and understanding, fostering a more inclusive work environment.

2. Flexible Work Arrangements: Implement flexible work policies that accommodate diverse cultural attitudes towards time and work-life balance. Flexibility in work hours and remote work options can enhance employee satisfaction and productivity.

3. Performance-Based Metrics: Focus on results-driven performance evaluations rather than rigid adherence to schedules. Emphasize productivity, quality of work, and goal achievement over the time spent in the office.

4. Inclusive Policies: Develop policies that promote diversity and inclusion, recognizing and valuing the unique contributions of employees from different cultural backgrounds.

5. Employee Engagement: Foster a supportive and engaging work environment through regular communication, team-building activities, and opportunities for professional development.

6. Health and Well-Being: Prioritize employee health and well-being through wellness programs, mental health support, and initiatives that promote work-life balance.

By integrating these best practices into HR strategies, organizations can navigate the complexities of cultural differences, creating a more cohesive and effective global workforce.

Future Trends and Insights

As globalization continues to shape the business landscape, HR professionals must stay ahead of emerging trends and challenges. The future of HR will likely see increased reliance on technology, data analytics, and artificial intelligence to manage and optimize workforce behavior. However, the human element of HR—understanding and respecting cultural differences—will remain paramount.

Technology and Data Analytics

The use of technology and data analytics in HR is transforming how organizations manage their workforce. Predictive analytics can help identify trends in employee behavior, such as patterns of tardiness or absenteeism, allowing HR to address issues proactively. Additionally, HR technology platforms can facilitate flexible work arrangements and remote collaboration, supporting global teams.

Artificial Intelligence

Artificial intelligence (AI) is being increasingly used to enhance HR processes, from recruitment to performance management, succession planning, and separation, as well as corporate social responsibility (CSR). AI can provide personalized training and development programs, tailored to individual needs and cultural contexts. However, HR professionals must ensure that AI is used ethically and that its implementation considers cultural sensitivities.

Cultural Intelligence

Cultural intelligence (CQ) will become a critical competency for HR professionals in the globalized workplace. CQ involves understanding and adapting to different cultural contexts, enabling HR to develop more effective and inclusive strategies. Investing in cultural intelligence training for HR teams can enhance their ability to navigate cultural differences and improve organizational performance.

Remote and Hybrid Work

The shift towards remote and hybrid work models, accelerated by the COVID-19 pandemic, will continue to influence HR practices. Organizations must develop policies that support remote work while maintaining productivity and engagement. This includes providing the necessary technology, fostering virtual collaboration, and ensuring that remote employees feel connected to the organization.

The global HR climate is dynamic and multifaceted, shaped by cultural, social, and technological forces. By understanding and respecting cultural differences, HR professionals can create strategies that enhance employee satisfaction, productivity, and organizational performance. As the world becomes more interconnected, the ability to navigate cultural nuances will be a key driver of success for the global workforce.

"True transformation begins with understanding the roots of culture and daring to evolve. When organizations align their values with cultural shifts, they unlock the power to lead with purpose and vision."

Chapter 2

Transforming Organizational Culture:

Lessons from Saudi Arabia's Cultural Shift

In recent years, Saudi Arabia has embarked on a monumental journey to transform its national culture, moving towards greater liberalization, openness, and societal freedom. This ambitious shift, spearheaded by strategic government initiatives, showcases the profound impact of determined leadership and well-structured policies in reshaping societal norms. HR professionals can draw invaluable lessons from Saudi Arabia's cultural evolution to drive significant changes within their organizations, even with limited resources.

The Crown Prince's Vision 2030: A Cultural Shift

Vision 2030, launched in 2016, is an ambitious reform program aimed at transforming Saudi Arabia into a more diversified, innovative, and modern economy. At the heart of these reforms is a cultural shift aimed at loosening social restrictions, empowering women, and encouraging foreign investment. These changes are not only economic but deeply cultural, as the government seeks to shift the nation's mindset from a traditional, conservative outlook to one that is more open, innovative, and globally competitive.

Some key changes include:

- Women's Empowerment: The lifting of the driving ban for women and the opening up of more job opportunities for women across various sectors.
- Workplace Modernization: Encouraging a more open, performance-driven workplace culture by promoting the inclusion of women and younger workers in decision-making roles.
- Diversification of the Economy: Developing sectors such as tourism, entertainment, and technology to reduce the country's dependence on oil.

The Saudi Arabian Transformation: A Case Study

Saudi Arabia's Vision 2030, championed by Crown Prince Mohammed bin Salman, serves as a comprehensive blueprint for economic diversification and social reforms. This visionary initiative includes promoting gender equality, expanding cultural and entertainment sectors, and opening the country to international tourism and business. The successful execution of these reforms hinges on clear communication, robust policies, and the engagement of influential leaders to inspire and drive societal transformation.

Key Lessons for HR: Leading Organizational Change

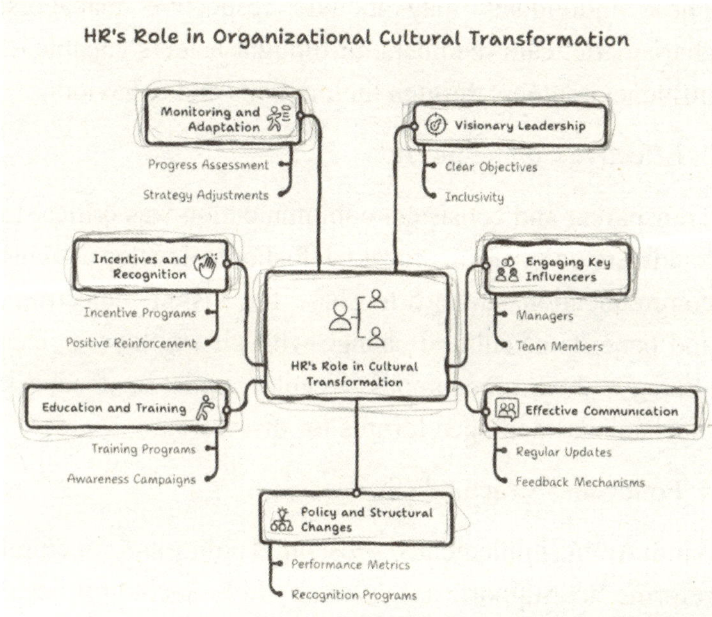

1. Visionary Leadership and Clear Objectives

Just as Saudi Arabia's Vision 2030 outlined a clear roadmap for national transformation, HR should articulate a compelling vision for the desired organizational culture. This vision should define specific goals such as fostering inclusivity, enhancing collaboration, or promoting innovation.

2. Engaging Key Influencers

In Saudi Arabia, influential leaders have played a crucial role in advocating for cultural change. Similarly, HR should identify and empower key influencers within the organization who can champion the cultural transformation. These individuals may include respective managers, charismatic team members, or thought leaders capable of influencing others through their actions and behaviors.

3. Effective Communication

Transparent and consistent communication was critical to Saudi Arabia's reform process. HR should develop a robust communication strategy to share the vision, objectives, and benefits of cultural change with all employees. This strategy should encompass regular updates, feedback mechanisms, and open forums for discussion.

4. Policy and Structural Changes

Saudi Arabia implemented substantial policy and structural reforms to support its cultural shift, including legal reforms and investments in new industries. HR should similarly revise organizational policies and procedures to align with the desired culture. This may involve updating performance metrics, recognition programs, and organizational structures to reinforce new cultural norms.

5. Education and Training

Education and awareness campaigns played a pivotal role in changing public perceptions in Saudi Arabia. HR should design and implement training programs that educate employees about new cultural expectations, equipping them with the necessary skills, knowledge and behaviours to embrace and contribute to organizational transformation.

6. Incentives and Recognition

Recognizing and rewarding behaviors that align with new cultural values is essential. HR should establish incentive programs that celebrate individuals and teams demonstrating desired cultural traits. By doing so, HR reinforces positive behaviors and motivates others to follow suit.

7. Monitoring and Adaptation

Continuous monitoring and agility in adapting to strategies was crucial to Saudi Arabia's ongoing cultural shift. HR should implement mechanisms to regularly assess the progress of cultural transformation, gather feedback, and make necessary adjustments to strategies and initiatives to ensure sustained momentum and success.

Lessons for Organizational Cultural Change

The culture shift in Saudi Arabia offers a powerful lesson for organizations looking to transform their own cultures. While government-led reforms provided the necessary framework for change, it was the deliberate focus on HR policies and practices that made the transition effective. Here's how organizations can follow suit:

1. Leadership Commitment and Vision

The culture change, whether at the national or organizational level, begins with leadership. Just as Crown Prince Mohammed bin Salman outlined a clear vision for the future of Saudi Arabia, organizational leaders must articulate a compelling vision for change. Leaders need to communicate why change is necessary and what the desired outcomes will be, ensuring that employees understand the bigger picture and how it aligns with their own roles.

HR's Role:

HR professionals should collaborate with leadership to develop a clear and inclusive communication strategy, ensuring that the vision for culture change is communicated effectively at all levels. This includes regular updates, workshops, and one-on-one discussions to align employees with the organizational goals.

2. Empowerment of Marginalized Groups

A key aspect of Saudi Arabia's cultural shift was the empowerment of women and young professionals—groups that had previously been underrepresented in the workforce. By lifting restrictions and promoting equality, the government set a precedent for organizations to follow.

HR's Role:

HR departments must ensure that policies are in place to promote diversity and inclusion within the organization. This includes providing equal opportunities for underrepresented groups, creating mentorship programs, and actively encouraging participation in leadership roles. Empowerment is about ensuring that all employees feel valued and have the opportunity to contribute meaningfully.

3. Modernizing Workplace Practices

Saudi Arabia's Vision 2030 focuses on fostering innovation and global competitiveness, which requires organizations to shift away from traditional, hierarchical structures toward more dynamic, agile, and wide-span models. This has included promoting a performance-based work culture and adopting international best practices in talent management.

HR's Role:

HR can facilitate this transition by modernizing workplace policies. For example, HR can introduce flexible work hours, remote work options, and performance-based evaluations. Additionally, HR should focus on upskilling the workforce by offering continuous training and development programs to ensure that employees possess the necessary skills to adapt to modern work environments.

4. Building a Culture of Innovation

One of the most significant cultural shifts in Saudi Arabia is the emphasis on innovation. From the development of new industries such as technology and entertainment to the promotion of entrepreneurship, Saudi Arabia is positioning itself as a hub for creativity and innovation.

HR's Role:

HR can foster a culture of innovation within the organization by encouraging experimentation and rewarding creative thinking. This includes creating safe spaces where employees can pitch new ideas without fear of failure. HR can also promote cross-functional collaboration and knowledge sharing to stimulate innovation.

5. Aligning Cultural Change with Economic Goals

The cultural changes in Saudi Arabia were closely aligned with the country's economic objectives, including reducing its dependence on oil and diversifying the economy. Similarly, in organizations, cultural change should be tied to clear business objectives. This alignment ensures that cultural shifts are not seen as isolated HR initiatives but as integral to the organization's overall success.

HR's Role:

HR professionals should work with leadership to ensure that cultural change initiatives are aligned with the organization's strategic goals. For example, if an organization is moving toward a more customer-centric model, HR should focus on cultivating a culture that prioritizes customer service excellence.

Case Study: Cultural Transformation in a Saudi Arabian Technology Firm

A leading technology firm in Saudi Arabia sought to modernize its corporate culture in alignment with the broader objectives of Vision 2030. The company's leadership, recognizing the need for change, worked closely with the HR department to drive this transformation.

The firm had traditionally operated with a hierarchical,

top-down management style, with limited opportunities for women and young employees to contribute to decision-making. In alignment with Vision 2030, the HR department implemented several initiatives:

- Inclusive Recruitment: The HR team set clear targets for increasing female representation in the workforce, particularly in leadership roles.
- Innovation Hubs: HR launched internal innovation hubs, where employees could collaborate on new ideas and projects, fostering a more dynamic and creative work environment.
- Flexible Work Policies: The company introduced flexible working hours and performance-based rewards, moving away from rigid, time-based evaluations.

As a result, the company saw a significant improvement in employee engagement, productivity, and retention rates. The cultural shift not only made the organization more innovative and competitive but also helped it align more closely with Saudi Arabia's national vision.

Saudi Arabia's Cultural Shift: Historical and Contemporary Perspectives

Saudi Arabia's transition to liberalization and openness represents not only a modernization effort but also a strategic alignment with global norms while preserving cultural heritage. This section offers an in-depth analysis of the historical context and the transformative steps taken to achieve this cultural evolution.

Historical Context and Cultural Conservatism

Historically, Saudi Arabia has been renowned for its conservative societal norms, governed by strict adherence to Islamic principles. Key aspects of the traditional cultural landscape included:

- Gender Segregation: Segregation of men and women in public spaces and limited opportunities for women in education and employment.
- Restrictions on Entertainment: Limited availability of cinemas, concerts, and public celebrations.
- Economic Dependence on Oil: Heavy reliance on oil exports, with minimal diversification into other economic sectors.

Vision 2030: Catalyst for Change

Launched in 2016, Vision 2030 marked a significant turning point in Saudi Arabia's trajectory. This transformative vision encompassed several pivotal objectives:

- Economic Diversification: Reducing dependence on oil revenue by developing non-oil sectors such as tourism, entertainment, and technology.
- Social Reforms: Enhancing the role of women in society, expanding cultural and recreational opportunities, and fostering a more inclusive societal framework.
- International Integration: Opening the country to international investment, tourism, and enhancing Saudi Arabia's global image.

Implementation and Impact

1. Women's Empowerment:

    - Granting women the right to drive and actively participate in the workforce.
    - Appointing women to prominent positions in government and business sectors.

Example: Princess Reema bint Bandar's appointment as Saudi Arabia's ambassador to the United States exemplifies the increasing empowerment of women in leadership roles, signalling a paradigm shift in gender dynamics within the kingdom.

2. Cultural Initiatives:

- Reopening cinemas and hosting international cultural events and entertainment.
- Establishment of the General Entertainment Authority to oversee the expansion of cultural activities.

Case Study: The Saudi Seasons initiative, featuring diverse festivals and events across the nation, has significantly boosted tourism and local economies. Riyadh Season 2019, for instance, showcased international artists, sports events, and cultural festivals, illustrating Saudi Arabia's newfound cultural openness.

3. Economic Reforms:

- Creation of the Public Investment Fund (PIF) to invest in non-oil sectors.
- Launch of mega-projects like NEOM, a futuristic city designed to attract global talent and investment.

"Our vision is a tolerant country, with Islam as its constitution and moderation as its method." – Crown Prince Mohammed bin Salman and is featured in the official Vision 2030 document of Saudi Arabia.

This vision was further elaborated during the Future Investment Initiative conference held in Riyadh in October 2017. In his address, Crown Prince Mohammed bin Salman emphasized the need to return to a more moderate form of Islam, stating:

"We are returning to what we were before—a country of moderate Islam that is open to all religions and to the world."

These economic reforms have yielded positive outcomes, including increased foreign investment and diversification of the national economic landscape beyond oil revenues.

Practical Application: Lessons from Saudi Arabia

The successful cultural transformation in Saudi Arabia underscores the importance of strategic planning, visionary leadership, and continuous adaptation. HR professionals can apply these principles to drive cultural change within their organizations.

Saudi Arabia's cultural transformation offers invaluable insights for HR professionals seeking to effect organizational change. By embracing visionary leadership, engaging key influencers, implementing effective communication strategies, and enacting policy and structural changes, HR can successfully drive significant cultural shifts within their organizations. Additionally, the importance of education and training, coupled with incentives and recognition, underscores the need for a comprehensive approach to fostering a dynamic and inclusive workplace.

Continuous monitoring and adaptation are essential to maintaining momentum and achieving sustainable transformation. As demonstrated by Saudi Arabia's Vision 2030, a clear roadmap, strategic initiatives, and the active involvement of influential leaders can lead to profound cultural changes. Organizations that adopt these principles can not only create a more inclusive and innovative environment but also position themselves to thrive in an increasingly diverse and globalized world.

Using the example of Saudi Arabia's cultural shift under Vision 2030 highlights the potential for large-scale cultural transformation, Yet, even with strong leadership and clear direction, many organizations still find it extremely difficult to change their internal cultures. Here's why:

1. Deeply Rooted Habits and Norms

Cultural norms, much like in Saudi Arabia before the reforms, are often deeply ingrained over years or even decades. In organizations, these norms shape how employees behave, interact, and make decisions. Long-standing beliefs, routines, and practices create a sense of stability and comfort. Employees, especially those who have been with the organization for a long time, may resist change because they are accustomed to the existing way of doing things.

In Saudi Arabia, for example, conservative traditions had been in place for generations, and while Vision 2030 brought about a shift, it wasn't easy for individuals and institutions to adjust. Similarly, in organizations, deeply embedded cultures cannot be shifted overnight—people need time to unlearn old habits and embrace new ones.

2. Resistance to Change

One of the most significant barriers to cultural change is the natural resistance people have to the change itself. Employees may be reluctant to alter their work habits or adopt new values, particularly if they feel the changes threaten their status, comfort, or security. In the case of Saudi Arabia's cultural reforms, the government faced resistance from more conservative factions of society who were hesitant to embrace a more modern and open cultural identity. Similarly, within organizations, employees—especially those in positions of power—may resist new cultural norms if they feel they undermine their influence.

3. Lack of Alignment with Leadership

In Saudi Arabia, Crown Prince Mohammed bin Salman's leadership was instrumental in advancing the cultural transformation. His clear vision and strong backing gave credibility to the reforms. In organizations, if leaders do not actively and consistently champion cultural change, employees are unlikely to adopt the new norms. Cultural change requires leadership to not only communicate the vision but also embody it through their own behaviours. If employees see a gap between what leaders say and what they do, change initiatives will fail.

4. Fear of the Unknown

Cultural change often requires employees to step into unfamiliar territory, which can create anxiety. In Saudi Arabia, as the workforce began to open up to women and younger professionals, there was concern about how this would impact traditional workplace dynamics. Similarly, in organizations, employees may worry about how changes in culture will affect their roles, relationships, or career progression. This fear of the unknown can lead to passive resistance, where employees may not openly oppose the change but fail to embrace it fully.

5. Subcultures within Organizations

Just as Saudi Arabia's Vision 2030 faced challenges in implementing reforms uniformly across a diverse population, organizations often have multiple subcultures—different departments, teams, or regions may have their own unique ways of doing things. This makes it difficult to implement a single cultural change across the entire organization. For example, a sales team might have a more aggressive, competitive culture, while the HR department may prioritize collaboration and empathy. Aligning these subcultures with the broader organizational change requires tailored approaches to each group.

6. Lack of Immediate Results

Cultural change takes time, and the lack of immediate, tangible results can cause frustration and disengagement among employees. In Saudi Arabia, Vision 2030's reforms are part of a long-term strategy, and while significant progress has been made, some changes are gradual. Similarly, in organizations, employees may expect quick results from cultural change initiatives, but when they don't see immediate improvements, they may lose motivation or revert to old behaviors.

7. Misalignment with Organizational Structures

For cultural change to succeed, the organization's structure, policies, and reward systems must support the desired culture. In Saudi Arabia, alongside cultural reforms, the government made structural changes to its legal and economic frameworks to support Vision 2030. In organizations, if the formal structures (like hierarchies, reward systems, and performance evaluations) do not align with the new cultural values, employees will be confused or skeptical about the change. For example, if an organization promotes a culture of innovation but continues to penalize failures and non-alignments, employees will hesitate to take risks.

The HR Role in Overcoming Challenges

HR plays a critical role in overcoming these barriers to cultural change. Drawing lessons from Saudi Arabia's Vision 2030, organizations must:

- Provide Strong Leadership Support: Ensure that leaders are visibly and actively supporting the change.

- Communicate the Vision Clearly: Just as Vision 2030 was communicated as a national transformation, organizations need a straightforward, compelling narrative for why the change is necessary.
- Address Resistance with Empathy: Understand the source of resistance and address the employees' concerns transparently.
- Create Alignment Across the Organization: Align policies, structures, and reward systems with the desired culture.
- Be Patient but Persistent: Cultural change is a long-term endeavor, and success comes with persistence and adaptability.

The challenges are significant, but with the right approach and strong leadership from HR, organizations can achieve lasting cultural transformation, just as Saudi Arabia has begun to accomplish through Vision 2030.

In summary, the lessons from Saudi Arabia's cultural shift underscore the potential for organizations to reevaluate and redefine their cultural landscapes. By drawing parallels and implementing tailored strategies, HR professionals can lead their organizations through successful cultural transformations, ensuring alignment with evolving societal and global expectations. This approach not only enhances organizational resilience and adaptability but also fosters a culture of continuous improvement and inclusivity, driving long-term success.

" Excellence thrives at the crossroads of tradition and innovation, where the relentless pursuit of perfection shapes both culture and enterprise."

CHAPTER 3

The European Commitment to Performance and Perfection:

Cultural Foundations and Organizational Impacts

Europe has long been admired for its strong commitment to excellence in performance, precision, and efficiency. This commitment permeates various sectors, from engineering, manufacturing, education, and healthcare. What is particularly striking about the European approach is that this focus on perfection and performance often begins in early childhood, with schools and families instilling values of discipline, precision, and accountability. The European approach to performance management and the pursuit of perfection in work are deeply ingrained cultural traits that manifest from childhood through adulthood. These habits are not arbitrary but are rooted in historical, educational, and social practices that emphasize discipline, precision, and a strong work ethic. This chapter examines the cultural foundations of these traits and their implications for human resource (HR) practices in European contexts.

Historical and Cultural Foundations:

Historical Context

Europe's history, marked by industrialization, scientific advancements, and cultural movements, has fostered a culture that values precision, innovation, and excellence. The legacies of the Enlightenment and the Industrial Revolution, for example, emphasized rationality, efficiency, and the pursuit of knowledge, laying the groundwork for a meticulous approach to work.

- Enlightenment Era: The Enlightenment, with its emphasis on reason and science, cultivated a culture of intellectual rigor and methodical thinking. This period saw the emergence of scientific methods and empirical research, setting standards for precision and thoroughness. Names worth mentioning are: Galileo Galilei, Isaac Newton, James Watt (from the Enlightenment and Scientific Revolution period); Archimedes (Ancient Greece, a precursor to scientific thought); and later figures inspired by Enlightenment ideals, such as Thomas Edison, Albert Einstein, and the Wright Brothers.
- Industrial Revolution: The Industrial Revolution brought about significant technological advancements and the establishment of manufacturing standards. The need for precision in production processes and the development of engineering disciplines further reinforced the value placed on meticulousness and high-quality work. Names worth mentioning are: Frederick

Taylor, Henri Fayol, Maslow, Herzberg, Joseph Juran, and W. Edwards Deming, who emerged between the late 19th and mid-20th century, significantly shaping management thought and quality practices during and after the Industrial Revolution.

Cultural Foundations: Precision and Performance from Childhood

In many European countries, children are taught from an early age to value accuracy and attention to detail. The education system, especially in countries such as Germany, Switzerland, and the Netherlands, emphasizes structure, discipline, and high standards. Even in simple tasks such as making sure the corners of a piece of paper align perfectly in schoolwork, children are exposed to the idea that precision is important—not just in academic tasks but in all aspects of life.

This meticulous attention to detail, cultivated from early childhood, lays the foundation for the performance-driven culture seen in European workplaces. Students grow up with the understanding that excellence is not optional—it is a responsibility. For instance, in Germany, the dual education system combines academic learning with practical apprenticeships, fostering a culture of precision and efficiency. In Switzerland, students follow vocational pathways that emphasize punctuality and accuracy, traits reflected in the country's world-class watchmaking and banking industries. In Finland, even with a creative and student-centered approach, schools instill strong values of personal responsibility and quality, shaping a workforce known for innovation and high standards. Meanwhile, in France, the competitive academic environment, especially in the grandes écoles, cultivates discipline and meticulousness among future leaders in engineering, administration, and public policy.

Case Study: German Education and Precision

In Germany, precision is an integral part of the education system, where even the most minor tasks are given serious attention. For example, in elementary schools, children are taught to organize their work neatly. Teachers encourage them to fold papers perfectly, ensuring all four corners align, and to write with accuracy and clarity. These tasks, while seemingly minor, instill a mindset that values precision and order.

As these children grow into professionals, this focus on precision is evident in the workplace. German engineers, for instance, are known worldwide for their meticulous approach to problem-solving and innovation. This level of attention to detail is not something that is learned in adulthood; it is cultivated over years of disciplined practice.

Educational Systems: Performance-Oriented

Beyond teaching precision, European education systems also promote a strong performance orientation. Students are encouraged to take responsibility for their learning, with many European schools emphasizing self-regulation and accountability from a young age. In countries like Finland and Sweden, students are taught how to manage their own time, set goals, and assess their progress—skills that are essential for performance-oriented workplaces.

Example: Swiss Approach to Apprenticeships

Switzerland's renowned apprenticeship system is a prime example of how performance orientation is integrated into education. Students in Switzerland typically begin apprenticeships at the age of 15 or 16, combining school education with practical work experience. This model instills a strong work ethic and an understanding of how high performance is linked to success in the professional world.

The emphasis is on delivering quality outcomes, being disciplined, and continuously improving performance. Swiss apprenticeships demand accountability from students, requiring them to meet professional standards while still completing their education. This early exposure to workplace demands shapes Swiss professionals into individuals who value precision, performance, and perfection.

European educational systems often emphasize rigorous academic standards, critical thinking, and attention to detail from a young age. In countries like Germany, the educational approach includes a combination of theoretical knowledge and practical skills, promoting thoroughness and precision. Students are encouraged to take pride in their work and to strive for high standards, whether in academics, crafts, or extracurricular activities.

Early Education: From primary school, European students are taught the importance of discipline, punctuality, and responsibility. Homework and classroom assignments are designed to cultivate attention to detail and a strong work ethic.

Vocational Training: In Germany, the dual vocational training system integrates academic learning with practical experience, ensuring that students acquire both theoretical knowledge and hands-on skills. This approach produces highly skilled professionals who are meticulous and reliable.

Social Norms and Values

Social norms in many European countries place a high value on reliability, punctuality, and responsibility. From childhood, individuals are taught to respect rules, adhere to schedules, and take their responsibilities seriously. These values translate into professional environments where employees are expected to consistently deliver high-quality work.

- Punctuality and Reliability: Punctuality is a deeply ingrained social expectation in many European cultures. Being on time is seen as a sign of respect and professionalism, and reliability is a cornerstone of personal and professional relationships.

- Work-Life Balance: While Europeans value hard work and precision, they also emphasize the importance of a balanced lifestyle. This balance ensures that employees are productive and focused during work hours, contributing to overall efficiency and quality.

The German Example: Precision and Thoroughness

The German culture provides a particularly striking example of these traits. Known for their engineering excellence, meticulous planning, and quality craftsmanship, Germans exhibit a strong aversion to taking shortcuts. A few examples are companies like Siemens and Bayer. This cultural characteristic is evident in everyday tasks, such as making a precise paper square fold, and extends to professional settings.

Education and Training

The German education system, with its dual vocational training programs, combines classroom instruction with hands-on experience. This approach instills a strong sense of discipline and attention to detail in students, preparing them for the demands of the workforce. The emphasis on quality and precision is reinforced through apprenticeships and professional training.

Work Ethic and Professionalism

In the workplace, Germans are renowned for their punctuality, thoroughness, and dedication to producing high-quality work. This work ethic is supported by organizational structures that prioritize clear processes, detailed planning, and continuous improvement. The cultural aversion to shortcuts ensures that tasks are completed correctly and thoroughly, reflecting a broader societal commitment to excellence.

Case Study: Volkswagen Group

Volkswagen, one of Germany's largest automotive manufacturers, exemplifies the German commitment to precision and quality. The company's rigorous engineering standards and meticulous production processes have established its reputation for reliability and innovation. Volkswagen's success can be attributed to its systematic approach to quality control, continuous improvement, and investment in employee training and development.

Implications for HR Practices

Understanding the cultural foundations of performance management and perfectionism in Europe has significant implications for HR practices. HR professionals can leverage these cultural traits to foster a high-performing and quality-focused organizational culture.

Performance Management Systems

European organizations often implement robust performance management systems that emphasize clear goals, regular feedback, and continuous development. These systems, one of which is the Balance scorecard, are designed to support employees in achieving high standards and improving their skills over time. HR can enhance these systems by incorporating structured performance reviews, personalized development plans, and targeted training programs.

Quality Assurance and Continuous Improvement

The cultural emphasis on precision and thoroughness aligns well with quality assurance practices and continuous improvement initiatives. ISO-9000 lays down strict adherence to prescribed management practices. HR can promote these practices by encouraging a culture of accountability, recognizing and rewarding high-quality work, and implementing processes that support ongoing learning and development.

Training and Development

Investing in comprehensive training and development programs is essential to maintaining high standards of performance. HR should design programs that reinforce attention to detail, problem-solving skills, and a commitment to quality. This includes technical training, leadership development, and opportunities for cross-functional collaboration.

Cultural Sensitivity and Adaptation

For multinational organizations, understanding and respecting these cultural traits are crucial when managing diverse teams. HR should develop culturally sensitive policies and practices that acknowledge the unique strengths of European employees while fostering collaboration and cohesion across different cultural contexts.

Case Study: Siemens AG

Siemens, a leading global technology company headquartered in Germany, exemplifies the integration of cultural traits into HR practices. Siemens emphasizes continuous learning and quality improvement through its comprehensive training programs and performance management systems. The company's commitment to precision and innovation is evident in its high standards for employee performance and product quality.

Perfectionism and Innovation: The Balancing Act

While perfectionism can be a strength in terms of producing high-quality work, it can also stifle innovation if taken to extremes. European countries, especially those in Scandinavia, have found a way to strike a balance between the drive for perfection and the need for creativity and innovation. In countries like Denmark and Norway, workplaces are designed to foster collaboration and experimentation, while still maintaining high standards of performance.

In these countries, the education system fosters both the drive for excellence and the ability to innovate. From a young age, students are encouraged to solve problems creatively while ensuring that their solutions are both practical and effective. This combination of creativity and precision enables European organizations to lead in industries such as automotive engineering and pharmaceuticals, where both innovation and accuracy are paramount.

Case Study: Finnish Educational Practices

Finland is often hailed as having one of the best education systems in the world. Finnish schools emphasize both independent learning and accountability, allowing students to take ownership of their progress. From an early age, students are taught not only to meet high performance standards but also to embrace a growth mindset—

acknowledging that learning from failure is a key part of achieving perfection.

This approach translates into a highly innovative and adaptable workforce. Finland is home to companies like Nokia and Rovio (creator of Angry Birds), which exemplify how a commitment to performance can coexist with a culture of creativity. The Finnish model shows that performance does not have to be rigid or stifling—when balanced with innovation, it can drive both personal and organizational success.

Building a Performance-Driven Workforce: The Role of HR

The European commitment to performance and perfection offers valuable lessons for HR professionals worldwide. While European organizations benefit from culturally ingrained values of precision, accountability, and high standards, HR teams must still actively cultivate these traits within the workforce.

1. Fostering a Culture of Accountability

HR can implement performance management systems that hold employees accountable for their work without micromanaging them. Providing regular feedback, setting clear goals, and offering opportunities for self-assessment help employees maintain high standards while developing a sense of ownership over their performance.

2. Promoting Lifelong Learning and Continuous Improvement

In Europe, particularly in countries like Germany and France, there is a strong emphasis on lifelong learning. HR can promote a similar culture by offering continuous development opportunities, that encourage employees to refine their skills and knowledge throughout their careers. This not only enhances individual performance but also benefits the organization as a whole.

3. Balancing Precision with Flexibility

While maintaining high standards is essential, HR must also ensure that the drive for perfection does not become paralyzing. HR can introduce flexible work environments that encourage experimentation and innovation while maintaining a commitment to quality. This balance is key to ensuring that the pursuit of perfection fosters creativity rather than stifling it.

Practical Steps for HR: Implementing Cultural Change

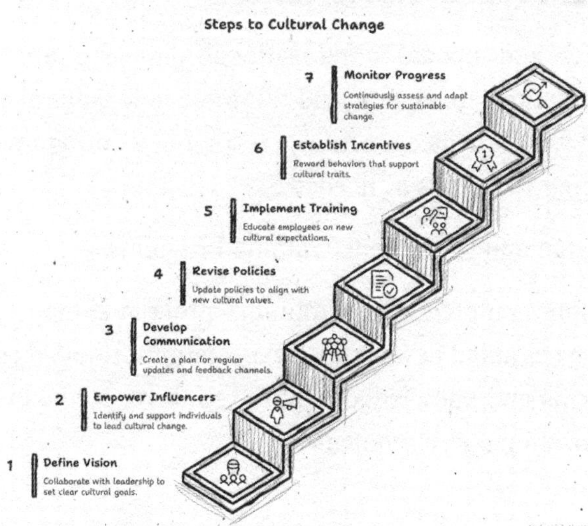

1. Define the Vision and Goals

Collaborate with senior leadership to define a clear vision for the desired organizational culture. Establish measurable goals that reflect this vision, ensuring alignment with broader organizational objectives.

2. Identify and Empower Influencers

Identify influential individuals within the organization who can serve as cultural ambassadors. Empower them with the necessary tools and support to lead by example and inspire others.

3. Develop a Communication Plan

Develop a comprehensive communication plan that includes regular updates, open forums, and designated channels for feedback. Ensure all employees are informed and engaged throughout the cultural transformation journey.

4. Update Policies and Procedures

Review and update organizational policies, procedures, and structures to support and reinforce new cultural values. Adapt performance metrics, recognition programs, and reporting structures as needed.

5. Design and Implement Training Programs

Develop comprehensive training programs that educate employees about new cultural expectations. Equip them with the skills and knowledge required to thrive in the evolving organizational environment.

6. Curate & Establish Incentive Programs

Implement recognition and incentive programs that reward behaviors and achievements aligned with desired cultural traits. Foster a culture where employees are motivated to embody and promote organizational values.

7. Monitor Progress and Adapt Strategies

Continuously monitor the progress of cultural change initiatives. Gather feedback from employees and stakeholders to assess effectiveness and identify areas for improvement. Adapt strategies as necessary to maintain momentum and achieve sustainable cultural transformation.

The European commitment to performance management and perfection is deeply rooted in cultural, historical, and educational practices. The lasting impact of early lessons plays a long-lasting role in shaping the culture. From the moment children enter school, they are taught the importance of doing things well, paying attention to detail, and taking responsibility for their own success. These values, cultivated in childhood, translate into the workplace and contribute to Europe's reputation for excellence in various industries. By understanding these foundations, HR professionals can implement strategies that harness these cultural strengths to drive organizational excellence. Emphasizing performance management, quality assurance, and continuous improvement can lead to a high-performing and quality-focused organizational culture, ultimately contributing to sustained success in the competitive global landscape.

"Rooted in tradition, precision-driven cultures set the benchmark for HR excellence, shaping the future of global progress."

CHAPTER 4

Global Progress through Performance-Driven HR Climates:

A Comparative Analysis

Human resources plays a pivotal role in driving organizational success, particularly in the context of globalization, where performance-oriented climates are essential for maintaining competitiveness. Across the globe, organizations are adopting performance-driven human resources (HR) strategies to align their workforces with broader business goals. As organizations around the world seek to enhance their competitive edge, the integration of performance-driven HR climates becomes increasingly critical. Countries and continents that embrace rigorous performance management, quality assurance, and continuous improvement are likely to see substantial progress in various sectors.

This chapter examines the regions poised for success under such HR climates and explores the reasons behind their potential for advancement that prioritizes performance, exploring the strengths and challenges of these approaches.

Global Perspectives on Performance-Driven HR Climates:

In different parts of the world, the approach to performance-driven HR climates varies significantly. While some regions emphasize metrics and quantifiable outcomes, others focus on holistic development and long-term growth. The cultural context greatly influences how performance is defined, measured, and rewarded.

Europe: The Precision and Efficiency Advantage

Germany

European countries adopt a more balanced approach to performance-driven HR climates. For instance, in Germany performance is essential, but it is not pursued at the expense of employee well-being. There is a strong emphasis on teamwork, collective success, and job security. European companies often invest heavily in employee development, ensuring that their workforce is equipped with the skills necessary to meet future challenges.

Germany's meticulous approach to work and strong emphasis on quality and precision make it a prime candidate for thriving under a performance-driven HR climate. The country's robust educational system, vocational training, and industrial expertise position it well to leverage HR practices that focus on performance and continuous improvement.

Performance Management in Practice: German companies, such as Siemens and Volkswagen, implement rigorous performance management systems that include clear goal setting, continuous feedback, and comprehensive employee training programs. These systems are designed to ensure that employees understand their roles and responsibilities clearly and are equipped with the skills needed to meet high standards of performance.

Case Study: At Siemens, performance reviews are conducted semi-annually, focusing on both results and behaviors. Employees are assessed against specific objectives and competencies, and development plans are created to address any gaps. This approach ensures a continuous cycle of performance improvement and professional growth.

France

In France, labour laws are designed to protect employees' rights, with restrictions on working hours and robust benefits programs. While this may seem to limit performance-driven initiatives, it fosters a more sustainable, long-term approach to productivity. Employees in Europe are encouraged to maintain a healthy work-life balance, which often leads to higher overall job satisfaction and , in turn, boosts long-term performance.

Scandinavia (Sweden, Denmark, Norway, Finland)

The Scandinavian countries are renowned for their robust social welfare systems, high standards of education, and emphasis on achieving a work-life balance. These nations can capitalize on performance-driven HR climates by integrating their existing focus on employee well-being with rigorous performance management, fostering innovation, and maintaining high productivity levels.

Performance Management in Practice: Companies in Scandinavia, such as IKEA and Novo Nordisk, implement performance management systems that emphasize employee engagement, continuous learning, and a balance between professional and personal life. These systems include regular performance discussions, personalized development plans, and flexible working arrangements.

"We believe that a healthy work-life balance is crucial for maintaining high levels of performance and innovation. Our performance management practices are designed to support our employees in achieving their professional goals while also enjoying a fulfilling personal life." – Lars Rebien Sørensen, former CEO of Novo Nordisk

Asia: The Rising Powerhouses

Japan

In Japan for instance, the concept of "Kaizen," or continuous improvement, is deeply embedded in workplace culture. HR practices focus on creating an environment where employees can continually enhance their skills and contribute to the company's overall success. However, this approach can lead to challenges, particularly in maintaining a work-life balance. In recent years, there has been growing awareness of the need to address overwork and burnout in Japanese companies, prompting HR departments to introduce more flexible working arrangements.

Japan's cultural emphasis on discipline, respect, and meticulousness aligns well with performance-driven HR practices. The country's history of industrial excellence, particularly in sectors such as automotive and electronics, demonstrates its ability to thrive under such conditions. Continuous improvement practices, such as Kaizen, already play a significant role in Japanese corporate culture.

Performance Management in Practice: Japanese companies, like Toyota and Sony, utilize performance management systems that integrate continuous improvement principles. Employees are encouraged to regularly assess their work processes and suggest improvements. Performance reviews are detailed and frequent, focusing on both individual contributions and team achievements.

Case Study: Toyota's implementation of the Kaizen philosophy in its performance management system has led to significant improvements in productivity and quality. Employees are trained to identify inefficiencies and propose solutions, fostering a culture of continuous improvement and excellence.

South Korea

In South Korea, performance-driven HR climates are reinforced through hierarchical organizational structures where respect for authority and seniority plays a key role. Employees are often expected to deliver beyond their official roles, contributing to team goals with a shared sense of responsibility. While this collectivist approach can enhance team cohesion and organizational loyalty, it can also suppress individual creativity and innovation if not carefully balanced by HR policies that encourage open communication and idea-sharing.

South Korea's rapid economic development and strong work ethic make it another strong candidate. The country's focus on education, technological advancement, and corporate discipline supports a performance-driven HR climate. South Korea's commitment to innovation and quality in industries like electronics and automotive further enhances its potential for progress.

Performance Management in Practice: South Korean companies, such as Samsung and Hyundai, emphasize performance management practices that focus on innovation, quality, and employee development. Regular performance reviews, targeted training programs, and a strong emphasis on results are key components of their HR strategies.

"Our commitment to innovation and quality is reflected in our performance management practices. We continuously invest in our employees' development to ensure they have the skills and knowledge needed to drive our success." – Lee Kun-hee, former Chairman of Samsung Group

North America: Innovation and Flexibility

United States

The United States' dynamic and diverse work culture, coupled with its emphasis on innovation and entrepreneurship, positions it well for progress under a performance-driven

HR climate. American companies often lead in developing cutting-edge technologies and management practices, and a focus on performance can drive further advancements in productivity and competitiveness.

Performance Management in Practice: Companies in the U.S., like Google and Microsoft, implement advanced performance management systems that emphasize innovation, collaboration, and continuous feedback. These systems include regular check-ins, 360-degree feedback, and data-driven performance metrics.

Case Study: Google's OKR (Objectives and Key Results) system is a hallmark of its performance management approach. Employees set ambitious goals and track their progress against key results, fostering a culture of high performance and accountability.

Canada

Canada's balanced approach to work-life integration, combined with its high educational standards and commitment to employee development, supports the implementation of performance-driven HR practices. The country's diverse and inclusive work environment can further enhance its ability to adapt and thrive under such climates.

Performance Management in Practice: Canadian companies, such as RBC (Royal Bank of Canada) and Shopify, focus on performance management systems that promote employee engagement, continuous learning, and diversity and inclusion. Regular performance reviews, personalized development plans, and inclusive policies are key features of their HR practices.

"We believe that a diverse and inclusive work environment is essential for driving high performance. Our performance management practices are designed to support all employees in achieving their full potential." – Tiff Macklem, Governor of the Bank of Canada

Latin America: Navigating Challenges to Performance

In Latin America, performance-driven HR climates are frequently influenced by external factors, including political instability and economic fluctuations. Despite these challenges, countries like Brazil and Mexico are increasingly adopting performance-based HR practices to improve competitiveness. Companies in these regions are focusing on performance appraisals, talent development, and leadership training to ensure that their workforce can meet global standards.

However, cultural factors, such as a strong emphasis on personal relationships and networks, can sometimes complicate performance-driven initiatives. In many Latin American countries, HR departments must strike a balance between maintaining strong interpersonal relationships and enforcing objective performance standards.

In Mexico, organizations are increasingly investing in leadership development programs to cultivate a performance-driven mindset among future leaders. These programs focus on developing strategic thinking, emotional intelligence, and adaptability—skills that are essential for navigating the region's often unpredictable business environment. By aligning leadership development with performance goals, Mexican companies are positioning themselves to compete more effectively on the global stage.

Oceania: The Balanced Approach

Australia

Australia's laid-back lifestyle does not preclude its potential for success in a performance-driven HR climate. The country's emphasis on work-life balance, combined with high standards of education and professional training, fosters a productive yet harmonious work environment. Australian organizations can leverage performance management to drive efficiency while maintaining employee satisfaction.

Performance Management in Practice: Australian companies, such as BHP and Commonwealth Bank, implement performance management systems that balance high performance with employee well-being. These systems include regular performance discussions, wellness programs, and flexible working arrangements.

Case Study: BHP's performance management approach includes regular goal-setting and feedback sessions, as well as programs that promote mental and physical well-being. This balanced approach has resulted in high levels of employee engagement and productivity.

Emerging Markets: Potential for Growth

China

China's rapid economic growth and significant investments in education and infrastructure provide a strong foundation for adopting performance-driven HR practices. While the cultural emphasis on hierarchy and conformity may pose challenges, the country's focus on technological advancement and industrial productivity aligns well with rigorous performance management.

Performance Management in Practice: Chinese companies, such as Huawei and Alibaba, implement performance management systems that emphasize efficiency, innovation, and results. These systems include regular performance reviews, key performance indicators (KPIs), and continuous improvement programs.

"Our performance management practices are designed to foster innovation and efficiency. We continuously invest in our employees' development to ensure they have the skills and knowledge needed to drive our success." – Ren Zhengfei, founder and CEO of Huawei

India

India's burgeoning tech and service industries, combined with a young and dynamic workforce, create a favorable environment for performance-driven HR climates. The country's educational institutions are increasingly focusing on skill development and professional training, which can support the adoption of performance-focused HR practices.

Performance Management in Practice: Indian companies, such as Tata Consultancy Services (TCS) and Infosys, implement performance management systems that emphasize employee development, innovation, and customer satisfaction. These systems include regular performance reviews, competency development programs, and rewards for high performance.

Case Study: Infosys' performance management system focuses on continuous learning and development. Employees undergo regular training and are encouraged to pursue certifications and advanced degrees, contributing to the company's reputation for excellence in the IT sector.

Countries and continents with strong educational systems, cultural emphasis on discipline and quality, and a commitment to continuous improvement are well-positioned to progress under performance-driven HR climates. Europe, with its precision and efficiency, Asia's rising powerhouses, North America's innovation and flexibility, Oceania's balanced approach, and emerging markets like China and India all demonstrate significant potential for success.

By adopting performance-driven HR practices, these regions can enhance their productivity, foster innovation, and maintain competitive advantages in the global market. The integration of such climates into organizational strategies will be key to achieving sustained progress and excellence in the increasingly interconnected and competitive world.

Challenges in Creating Performance-Driven Climates

While performance-driven HR climates have many benefits, they also present several challenges. Chief among them is the difficulty in balancing short-term performance with long-term sustainability. Organizations that focus too heavily on immediate results may experience high employee turnover, burnout, and a decline in job satisfaction. HR professionals must navigate these challenges by developing policies that promote both high performance and employee well-being.

1. Managing Expectations:

Employees in performance-driven climates often face immense pressure to meet targets, which can lead to stress and burnout. HR must work to set realistic goals and provide the necessary support systems—such as mental health resources, mentorship programs, and opportunities for career development.

2. Cultural Sensitivity:

Global organizations must recognize that a one-size-fits-all approach to performance-driven HR climate is unlikely to succeed. HR professionals must tailor their strategies to fit the cultural context of each region, taking into account differences in attitudes toward work, authority, and reward systems.

3. Incorporating Flexibility:

As the global workforce becomes more diverse and dynamic, HR professionals must introduce flexible performance management systems. This includes offering remote work options, flexible hours, and alternative forms of performance evaluation that cater to the varying needs of employees.

In summary, the comparative analysis of different countries' performance management practices illustrates the diverse approaches to achieving high standards of performance and quality. By understanding and leveraging these cultural and organizational strengths, HR professionals can design and implement effective performance management systems that drive continuous improvement and organizational success. Creating a performance-driven HR climate is essential for organizational success in today's competitive global market. However, HR professionals must strike a careful balance between promoting high performance and maintaining employee well-being. By tailoring performance management strategies to the cultural context of each region, organizations can foster a climate that not only drives results but also sustains long-term success and employee well-being.

"India's unparalleled HR strength stems from its traditional emotional connectivity, driving loyalty, unity, and transformative growth in a globalized world."

CHAPTER 5

The Power of Traditional Emotional Connectivity:

India's Unique HR Advantage

India's work culture is deeply intertwined with emotional connectivity, where personal relationships, family values, and mutual respect are critical components of organizational dynamics. This emotional fabric gives India a unique HR advantage, setting it apart from more transactional workplace cultures seen elsewhere in the world. At the heart of this lies the Indian tradition of strong familial bonds, respect for elders, and a sense of community.

In the rapidly evolving global business landscape, where technological advancements and competitive pressures often dominate the narrative, the importance of traditional emotional connectivity in the workplace cannot be overstated. In India, this cultural trait stands out as a significant HR advantage, fostering a sense of community, loyalty, and collective well-being that can drive organizational success.

This chapter examines the deeply rooted tradition of emotional connectivity in India, its impact on the workplace, and the benefits it brings to HR practices and organizational culture. In the HR context, these cultural norms translate into employee loyalty, commitment, and a cooperative work environment.

The Cultural Fabric of Emotional Connectivity in India

India's cultural and social fabric is woven with strong emotional ties and interpersonal relationships. This connectivity is evident in various aspects of Indian life, including family structures, social interactions, community activities, and religious practices. These cultural norms naturally extend into the workplace, influencing how employees interact, collaborate, and support each other.

1. Family-Oriented Society

Indian society places a high value on family and close-knit relationships. This emphasis on familial bonds translates into the workplace, where colleagues often view each other as extended family members. Such a perspective fosters a supportive and collaborative work environment.

Example: In many Indian companies, it is common for employees to celebrate festivals, birthdays, and personal milestones together, creating a familial atmosphere. For instance, Infosys organizes events where employees' families are invited to the campus, reinforcing the family-like bond within the organization.

2. Collectivist Culture

India's collectivist culture prioritizes group harmony and collective success over individual achievements. This cultural orientation encourages teamwork, mutual support, and a strong sense of belonging among employees, enhancing workplace cohesion and morale.

Case Study: Tata Group, one of India's largest conglomerates, exemplifies this collectivist approach. The company emphasizes community and teamwork in its corporate culture, fostering a strong sense of loyalty and collective responsibility among its employees.

3. Hospitality and Respect

Traditional Indian values of hospitality and respect for others contribute to a warm and welcoming workplace atmosphere. These values promote inclusivity and empathy, enabling employees to form meaningful connections with their peers and superiors.

Example: At Wipro, a leading IT services company, the practice of offering respectful greetings, such as "Namaste" is encouraged among employees, fostering a culture of mutual respect and warmth.

The Role of Family Values in Shaping Work Culture

Indian society places great emphasis on family, and this deeply ingrained respect for family values naturally spills over into the workplace. Employees often treat their teams and colleagues as extensions of their family, which fosters a sense of belonging and emotional security. These close-knit bonds create an environment where employees feel valued not just for their contributions but as individuals.

Example: Familial Bonds in the Workplace

In Indian organizations, it is not uncommon for managers to take a personal interest in the well-being of their employees. From checking on family matters to providing emotional support during personal crises, these gestures are deeply appreciated and reciprocated with loyalty and dedication. A manager who inquires about an employee's family situation during a difficult time is likely to build a stronger, more committed team.

This family-like connection extends beyond direct manager-employee relationships. Teams often operate like extended families, celebrating successes together and supporting one another through challenges. This cultural trait strengthens collaboration and builds a resilient workforce, as employees feel supported on a personal level.

Emotional Connectivity as a Retention Tool

One of the most potent advantages of emotional connectivity in Indian workplaces is its role in employee retention. While competitive compensation and career advancement opportunities are significant, employees in India often stay with organizations where they feel emotionally connected. This bond is vital in industries where turnover is high. HR professionals in India are aware of the role that emotional ties play in retaining employees and often create initiatives that nurture these connections.

Example: The Emotional Anchor in Indian Corporates

Large Indian conglomerates, such as the Tata Group, are known for fostering long-term loyalty by building emotional connections with their employees. Tata's HR practices include extensive support systems for employees and their families, such as healthcare, education, and welfare programs. The emotional connection that employees feel toward the company is often cited as a reason for Tata's low turnover rate, despite competitive offers from rival firms.

In family-owned businesses, emotional connections are even more pronounced, as many employees develop personal relationships with business owners. These bonds, combined with a shared sense of purpose, create a loyalty that goes beyond financial incentives.

The Importance of Respect and Hierarchy

In Indian organizations, respect for hierarchy is not just about authority—it is about mutual respect and emotional care. The relationship between seniors and juniors often mirrors that of elders and younger family members. This cultural norm creates a workplace dynamic where deference to authority is balanced with emotional support, guidance, and mentorship.

While this hierarchy can sometimes be rigid, it also serves as a stabilizing force, especially in times of uncertainty. Employees feel a strong sense of security knowing that their superiors will protect their interests, much like elders in a family do for younger members. This sense of emotional security encourages employees to stay committed to their organizations.

Case Study: Infosys and the Role of Emotional Connectivity in HR

Infosys, one of India's largest IT services companies, has long been recognized for its people-centric HR practices. The company actively fosters emotional connectivity by offering not just professional development but also personal support. From counselling services to programs that assist employees during personal crises, Infosys recognizes that emotionally connected employees are more likely to stay loyal, be productive, and contribute to the company's growth.

Infosys places particular emphasis on maintaining emotional connectivity during its onboarding process. New employees are paired with mentors who guide them not only through their professional development but also help them acclimatize to the company culture. This mentorship program builds a strong emotional foundation from the start, fostering loyalty and long-term commitment.

Community-Oriented Workplaces: The Collective Over the Individual

In Indian workplaces, there is a strong sense of community that transcends individual achievements. While Western work cultures often emphasize individual performance, Indian organizations tend to value collective success. Employees take pride in contributing to the larger goals of their teams, departments, and the organization as a whole. This sense of collective responsibility is emotionally fulfilling and encourages collaboration over competition.

Example: Team-Oriented Culture in Indian Manufacturing

In manufacturing sectors, such as those in Coimbatore or Chennai, employees often develop strong team-oriented cultures. They are emotionally invested in the success of their teams and tend to go beyond their job descriptions to ensure that collective goals are met. This collaborative spirit is nurtured through team-building activities, mutual respect, and shared responsibility, all of which are deeply rooted in Indian values of community and cooperation.

Advantages of Emotional Connectivity in HR Practices

1. Enhanced Employee Engagement and Loyalty

Emotional connectivity leads to higher levels of employee engagement and loyalty. When employees feel emotionally connected to their colleagues and the organization, they are more likely to be motivated, committed, and invested in their work. This reduces turnover rates and enhances overall job satisfaction.

The Social Exchange Theory posits that when employees perceive a high level of support and emotional investment from their organization, they are more likely to reciprocate with higher levels of engagement and loyalty.

2. Effective Communication and Collaboration

Strong interpersonal relationships facilitate open and effective communication. In an emotionally connected workplace, employees are more comfortable sharing ideas, providing feedback, and collaborating on projects. This improves problem-solving capabilities and drives innovation, because the trust factor is very high.

"In our company, the culture of open communication and emotional bonding among team members has significantly enhanced our collaborative efforts, leading to innovative solutions and a harmonious work environment." – Azim Premji, Founder of Wipro

3. Supportive Work Environment

A culture of emotional connectivity creates a supportive work environment where employees feel valued and understood. This supportive network can help individuals cope with stress, navigate challenges, and maintain a healthy work-life balance, ultimately boosting productivity and well-being.

Example: Marico, a leading consumer goods company in India, has implemented several initiatives to support employee well-being, including counseling services and stress management programs. These efforts create a nurturing work environment that prioritizes employees' emotional health.

4. Cultural Sensitivity and Inclusion

HR practices that leverage emotional connectivity promote cultural sensitivity and inclusion. Recognizing and valuing the diverse backgrounds and perspectives of employees fosters a sense of belonging and respect, enhancing organizational cohesion and performance.

Case Study: Mahindra & Mahindra's diversity and inclusion programs celebrate the cultural and regional diversity of its workforce, encouraging employees to share their unique perspectives and experiences, thereby fostering an inclusive workplace culture.

5. Conflict Resolution

Emotional bonds and mutual respect among employees contribute to more effective conflict resolution. In an environment where relationships are prioritized, conflicts are more likely to be resolved amicably and constructively, preserving workplace harmony.

Example: In companies like Infosys, mediation and conflict resolution programs emphasize empathy and understanding, helping employees constructively navigate disagreements.

Implementing Emotional Connectivity in HR Strategies

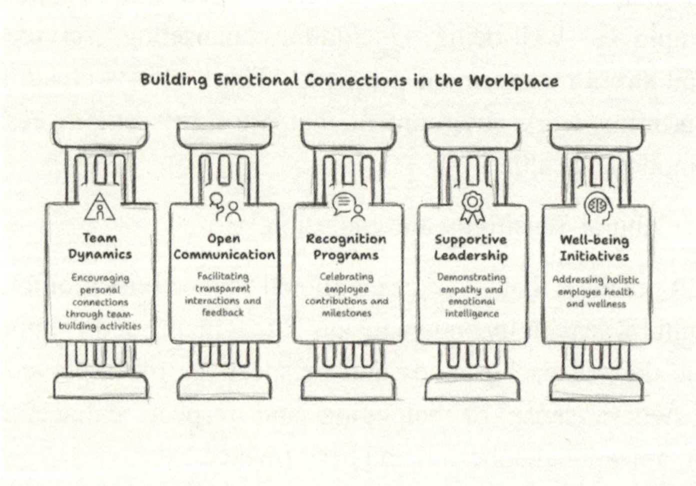

1. Building Strong Team Dynamics

HR can implement team-building activities and initiatives that encourage employees to connect on a personal level. Activities such as team outings, group projects, and celebrations during social events help strengthen interpersonal relationships and foster a sense of camaraderie.

Example : Infosys Technologies organizes regular off-site retreats and team-building exercises that allow employees to bond outside the office environment, strengthening team dynamics and improving collaboration.

2. Fostering Open Communication

Encouraging open communication channels and creating opportunities for employees to share their thoughts and feelings can enhance emotional connectivity. Regular feedback sessions, town hall meetings, and informal gatherings facilitate transparent and meaningful interactions.

Case Study: At Tata Consultancy Services (TCS), regular "Pulse Check" surveys are conducted to gauge employee sentiments and concerns. This feedback mechanism helps HR address issues promptly and maintain open lines of communication.

3. Recognition and Appreciation Programs

Implementing recognition and appreciation programs that celebrate employees' contributions and milestones reinforces a culture of respect and emotional connection. Personalized recognition and public acknowledgments of achievements can boost morale and strengthen bonds.

Example: Infosys' "Instep" program recognizes interns and employees for their outstanding contributions through personalized awards and public ceremonies, fostering a sense of appreciation and emotional connection.

4. Supportive Leadership

Leaders who demonstrate empathy, approachability, and emotional intelligence set the tone for a connected workplace. HR can provide training for leaders to develop these skills and encourage them to foster positive and supportive relationships with their teams.

"Empathy and emotional intelligence are crucial leadership traits. By demonstrating these qualities, leaders

can cultivate a supportive and connected workplace culture." – N. R. Narayana Murthy, Co-founder of Infosys

5. Well-being Initiatives

HR can introduce well-being initiatives that address employees' physical, mental, and emotional health. Programs such as counseling services, wellness workshops, and flexible work arrangements demonstrate that the organization values its employees' holistic well-being.

Case Study: Marico's "Wealthy Minds" initiative provides employees with access to mental health professionals, wellness resources, and workshops on stress management and work-life balance, underscoring the company's dedication to employee well-being.

Example of VIP Clothing Ltd.

VIP Clothing Ltd., a renowned name in the Indian apparel industry, stands as a shining example of how emotional connectivity can transform a workplace into a thriving community. The company has successfully integrated traditional Indian values into its operations, creating a unique work culture that prioritizes relationships alongside productivity. Employees often describe their workplace as a "second home," where colleagues are treated like members of an extended family. This emotional bond fosters a strong sense of belonging and encourages mutual respect among team members.

To nurture this family-like atmosphere, VIP Clothing Ltd. organizes regular cultural events, festival celebrations, and family get-togethers on Founders' Day. Festivals like Diwali, Pongal, Dussehra, Holi, and many others are celebrated with great enthusiasm, uniting employees across roles and departments in moments of shared joy. Additionally, the company invites employees' families to participate in events, further strengthening the bond between personal and professional life. These initiatives create an inclusive environment where employees feel valued, connected, and appreciated not just for their work but also as individuals.

The impact of this emotionally connected culture is profound. VIP Clothing Ltd. has cultivated a loyal workforce, with many employees dedicating decades of their lives to the organization. This deep sense of loyalty translates into higher morale, reduced turnover rates, and improved collaboration. By balancing traditional values with modern HR practices, VIP Clothing Ltd. proves that emotional connectivity in the workplace can drive both employee satisfaction and long-term organizational success.

HR's Role in Strengthening Emotional Connectivity

HR professionals in India have the unique task of nurturing emotional bonds in the workplace while maintaining professional boundaries. They play a crucial role in ensuring that emotional connectivity does not hinder performance but rather enhances it. HR initiatives in Indian organizations often include wellness programs, employee engagement activities, and opportunities for personal growth, all of which help strengthen the emotional ties between employees and the organization.

Wellness Programs: Indian organizations frequently offer wellness programs that address not just physical health but also emotional well-being. These programs may include mental health support, stress management workshops, and even family-oriented activities that strengthen the emotional connection employees have with their workplace.

Employee Engagement Activities: Festivals, family days, and team outings are common in Indian workplaces, providing opportunities for employees to bond on a personal level. HR professionals often use these events to foster a sense of belonging and emotional connection, ensuring that employees feel part of a larger community.

Recognition and Support: Emotional recognition plays a significant role in Indian HR practices. Employees are acknowledged not just for their performance but also for their personal contributions to team spirit and morale. Whether it's supporting a colleague during a difficult time or contributing to the workplace's emotional well-being, such actions are recognized and valued.

India's tradition of emotional connectivity offers a unique and powerful advantage in the realm of HR practices. By leveraging the deep-rooted cultural values of family orientation, collectivism, hospitality, and respect, organizations can create a workplace environment that fosters engagement, loyalty, and collaboration. Implementing HR strategies that prioritize emotional connectivity not only enhances individual and organizational performance but also contributes to a supportive and inclusive workplace culture.

In an era where human connections are often overshadowed by technological advancements, embracing the power of emotional connectivity can differentiate organizations and drive sustainable success. For India, this cultural trait is not just an advantage but a vital asset in building resilient, cohesive, and high-performing organizations. By integrating these traditional values into modern HR practices, Indian organizations can create workplaces that are not only productive but also nurturing and fulfilling, ensuring long-term success and employee satisfaction.

India's unique HR advantage lies in its ability to harness the power of emotional connectivity. The country's deep-rooted family values, respect for relationships, and emphasis on community create a workplace culture where employees feel emotionally connected and supported. For HR professionals, the challenge is to maintain these emotional bonds while driving organizational performance and competitiveness. By leveraging India's cultural strengths, HR can create a work environment that is both emotionally fulfilling and professionally rewarding.

"Relentless pace fuels unmatched efficiency and innovation, forging a future driven by ambition and resilience."

Chapter 6

The Fast-Paced Work Culture of East Asia:

Driving Efficiency and Innovation

East Asia is renowned for its fast-paced work environments, where efficiency, productivity, and innovation drive economic growth and organizational success. Countries like Japan, South Korea, China, and Taiwan have cultivated a workplace culture that prioritizes speed, precision, and continuous improvement. This rapid work ethic is not an accident but the product of cultural and educational systems that shape individuals from a young age. In East Asia, childhood upbringing and societal values contribute significantly to the development of a fast-paced, results-oriented workforce.

East Asia is renowned for its rapid economic development and technological advancements. Central to this progress is a distinctive work culture characterized by a fast-paced, high-pressure environment that prioritizes efficiency, productivity, and innovation.

This chapter examines the cultural, historical, and organizational factors that influence East Asia's fast-paced work culture, examining their implications for HR practices and organizational success. It provides detailed case studies to illustrate these principles in action.

Historical and Cultural Foundations

1. Historical Context

The rapid industrialization and economic reforms in East Asian countries have significantly influenced their work cultures. Post-World War II reconstruction in Japan, South Korea's economic miracle in the late 20th century, and China's economic liberalization since the 1980s have all fostered a sense of urgency and a drive for rapid development.

Example: Japan's post-war economic miracle, known as the "Japanese Economic Miracle," saw the country transform into a leading global economic power within a few decades. This period instilled a culture of hard work, efficiency, and innovation that endures to this day.

2. Confucian Values

Confucianism, which emphasizes respect for hierarchy, loyalty, and the collective good, has profoundly influenced East Asian work cultures. These values encourage employees to work diligently, respect authority, and prioritize organizational success over individual preferences.

"The superior man is modest in his speech but excels in his actions." – Confucius. This philosophy underpins the East Asian emphasis on action and results over rhetoric.

3. Educational Systems

East Asian educational systems are known for their rigor and high standards, preparing students for competitive and demanding work environments. The focus on discipline, hard work, and academic excellence creates a foundation for a fast-paced and performance-driven work culture.

Case Study: South Korea's education system, often described as hyper-competitive, produces a highly skilled and disciplined workforce. The rigorous academic environment instills a strong work ethic and a drive for success from a young age.

Characteristics of Fast-Paced Work Culture

1. High Expectations and Long Working Hours

East Asian workplaces are characterized by high expectations and long working hours. Employees often work beyond standard office hours to meet deadlines and achieve targets, reflecting a commitment to excellence and productivity.

Example: In Japan, the concept of "karoshi" (death from overwork) highlights the extreme lengths to which employees go to fulfill their duties. While this is an extreme example, it underscores the intense work ethic prevalent in Japanese culture.

2. Focus on Efficiency and Productivity

Efficiency and productivity are paramount in East Asian work cultures. Companies prioritize streamlined processes, continuous improvement, and technological innovation to maintain competitiveness and achieve rapid growth.

Theory: The "Kaizen" philosophy in Japan, which emphasizes continuous improvement, exemplifies this focus on efficiency. By encouraging small, incremental changes, organizations can enhance productivity and quality over time.

3. Emphasis on Innovation

East Asian countries are leaders in technological innovation, driven by a culture that encourages creativity and experimentation. This focus on innovation is supported by significant investments in research and development, as well as a willingness to take risks.

Case Study: China's rapid rise as a global leader in technology and innovation is a testament to its fast-paced work culture. Companies like Huawei and Alibaba have achieved global prominence through relentless innovation and a commitment to cutting-edge technology.

4. Hierarchical Structures

Despite the fast pace, East Asian work cultures often maintain hierarchical structures, where respect for authority and seniority are paramount. This hierarchy ensures clear lines of command and responsibility, facilitating efficient decision-making and execution.

Example: In South Korea, the concept of "nunchi," or reading the room, is essential in navigating hierarchical relationships. Employees are expected to understand and respond to the expectations of their superiors, contributing to organizational harmony and efficiency.

Case Studies of East Asian Work Culture

1. Case Study: Toyota's Kaizen Approach

Background: Toyota Motor Corporation, a global leader in the automotive industry, is renowned for its Kaizen (continuous improvement) approach. This philosophy encourages every employee, from factory workers to top executives, to suggest and implement small, incremental changes to improve efficiency and quality.

Implementation: Toyota's commitment to Kaizen involves regular training sessions, team meetings, and suggestion systems that empower employees to identify areas for improvement. This approach has led to significant enhancements in productivity, quality, and innovation.

Results: Toyota's Kaizen philosophy has led to streamlined production processes, reduced waste, and improved product quality. It has also fostered a culture of continuous learning and improvement, contributing to the company's long-term success.

2. Case Study: Samsung's Innovation-Driven Culture

Background: Samsung Electronics, a South Korean conglomerate, has emerged as a global leader in electronics and technology through its focus on innovation and efficiency. The company's fast-paced work culture emphasizes rapid product development, continuous improvement, and a commitment to excellence.

Implementation: Samsung invests heavily in research and development, with numerous innovation centers and labs dedicated to exploring new technologies and products. The company's performance management system rewards employees for innovative ideas and quick execution.

Results: Samsung's fast-paced work culture has led to groundbreaking innovations in consumer electronics, including smartphones, televisions, and semiconductors. The company's ability to quickly adapt to market changes and continuously innovate has solidified its position as a global leader.

3. Case Study: Alibaba's Entrepreneurial Spirit

Background: Alibaba Group, a Chinese multinational conglomerate specializing in e-commerce, technology, and retail, has built its success on a fast-paced, entrepreneurial work culture. Founded by Jack Ma, the company encourages risk-taking, creativity, and rapid execution.

Implementation: Alibaba fosters an entrepreneurial environment by empowering employees to take ownership of projects, experiment with new ideas, and learn from failures. The company's flat organizational structure and open communication channels support this dynamic culture.

Results: Alibaba's fast-paced work culture has driven its rapid growth and diversification into various sectors, including cloud computing, digital entertainment, and financial services. The company's ability to innovate and quickly scale new ventures has made it a dominant player in the global market.

Cultural Foundations: Speed and Discipline in Early Education

From an early age, children in East Asia are taught to value discipline, punctuality, and efficiency as foundational life skills. This cultural emphasis is deeply rooted in societal expectations and is evident in the education systems of countries like Japan and South Korea. In Japan, for instance, the idea that "time is money" is introduced to children as early as elementary school. Schools foster a structured environment where students learn to adhere to strict schedules, complete tasks efficiently, and maximize their time in the classroom. Teachers place a strong emphasis on balancing speed with quality, encouraging students to complete assignments quickly without compromising precision or thoroughness. This approach not only cultivates a sense of responsibility but also instills habits of time management and productivity from a young age.

Similarly, in South Korea, the educational system is known for its high degree of structure and rigor, which often rewards timeliness and efficiency. The competitive nature of schooling, particularly in the context of preparing for university entrance exams, pushes students to work swiftly and effectively under pressure. Time is treated as a valuable asset, and children are trained to navigate demanding schedules and prioritize their efforts toward achieving excellence. These early lessons in speed and discipline do not fade with age but rather evolve into professional expectations. As adults, South Koreans are accustomed to meeting tight deadlines and delivering high-quality results within constrained timelines, reflecting the values instilled during their formative years.

By emphasizing speed and discipline in education, these cultures prepare individuals not just for academic success but also for the challenges of a fast-paced, results-driven world. This foundational training shapes not only the individual's approach to tasks but also contributes to the broader efficiency and productivity observed in these societies.

Childhood Habits: A Culture of Speed and Urgency

In East Asia, children's daily routines and school experiences instill habits of fast-paced work and efficiency, which seamlessly translate into the professional world. From a young age, children are exposed to structures that prioritize discipline, time management, and collaboration. For instance, the tradition of early morning exercise routines, prevalent in countries such as Japan, China, and South Korea, encourages children to start their day with energy and focus. These exercises are often accompanied by rhythmic music or instructions, fostering a sense of collective purpose and urgency that carries into their studies and other daily tasks.

Educational Routines and Time-Bound Activities

In schools across East Asia, a strong emphasis is placed on efficiency through time-bound tasks and structured activities. Students are frequently given assignments with strict deadlines, teaching them to work quickly and manage their time effectively. These exercises are designed not only to develop individual skills but also to promote teamwork. Group activities and team-based projects are a staple of the classroom, emphasizing the importance of collaboration under tight schedules. These practices instill a sense of shared responsibility and highlight the value of working efficiently as a group, traits that are later reflected in the region's workplace culture.

Example: Japan's School Lunch Routine

A remarkable example of this culture of speed and organization can be observed in Japanese schools during lunchtime. The process of serving and eating lunch is not merely a break from studies; it is a carefully coordinated activity. Students take turns serving his or her classmates, ensuring that everyone receives his or her meal in an orderly and timely manner. This process is conducted within a fixed time frame, often involving cleaning up and returning to lessons immediately afterward. Such routines teach children to work efficiently within the confines of a schedule, reinforcing the importance of time management, cooperation, and respect for collective goals.

Example: Morning Ceremonies in Schools

In many East Asian schools, the day begins with a morning assembly or ceremony, during which students recite mottos, sing songs, or participate in quick team-building exercises. These ceremonies are highly structured and instill a sense of punctuality, discipline, and focus. Children learn from a young age to value every minute and align their actions with the broader goals of their group or institution.

This culture of speed and urgency, ingrained from early childhood, becomes a defining feature of adulthood in East Asia, where these habits contribute to the region's reputation for high productivity, meticulous time management, and collective harmony in the workplace.

The Role of Confucian Values in Shaping Work Culture

Confucianism, a dominant philosophical influence in many East Asian countries, emphasizes the importance of hard work, respect for authority, and the pursuit of excellence. These values have a direct impact on how individuals approach their professional lives. The emphasis on collective well-being over individualism fosters a culture where employees work diligently for the benefit of the organization as a whole.

In China, for example, the concept of "face" (or saving face) plays a critical role in maintaining personal and professional relationships. Individuals strive to avoid embarrassment or failure by working quickly and effectively, ensuring they meet or exceed expectations. This pressure to perform well is instilled in children from a young age, as they are encouraged to uphold family and societal honor through their achievements.

Case Study: Kaizen and Continuous Improvement in Japan

The Japanese concept of Kaizen, which means "continuous improvement," is a prime example of how cultural values drive innovation and efficiency in the workplace. Rooted in the idea that small, incremental changes can lead to significant improvements, Kaizen encourages employees to seek ways to optimize processes and reduce waste constantly. This philosophy is not limited to the workplace—it is introduced in schools, where students are taught to reflect on their performance and look for areas of improvement.

In manufacturing sectors, such as the automotive industry, Kaizen has been instrumental in driving efficiency and innovation. Companies like Toyota have adopted this philosophy, creating an environment where employees are encouraged to contribute ideas for improvement, no matter how small. This mindset of continuous improvement is deeply embedded in the culture and begins early in life, shaping the way individuals approach their work.

Fast-Paced Workplaces: The Influence of Technology and Globalization

The rise of technology and globalization has further accelerated the pace of work in East Asia. In countries such as South Korea and Taiwan, the tech industry is renowned for its rapid product development cycles and innovation pace. Employees in these sectors are expected to adapt quickly to new technologies and market demands, often working long hours to stay ahead of global competitors.

The drive for efficiency in these industries can be traced back to educational systems that emphasize the importance of mastering technology from a young age. In South Korea, for instance, coding and digital literacy are introduced in primary schools, preparing students to thrive in fast-paced, tech-driven environments. The ability to quickly learn and apply new skills is seen as essential for both personal and professional success.

Example: South Korea's "Palli Palli" Culture

In South Korea, the phrase "palli palli" (meaning "hurry hurry") is a reflection of the nation's fast-paced culture. This sense of urgency is embedded in daily life, from the speed of public transportation to the rapid service in restaurants. In the workplace, "palli palli" drives employees to work quickly and efficiently, often under tight deadlines. This cultural norm is reinforced from childhood, where students are taught the importance of completing tasks swiftly and maintaining a high level of productivity.

Challenges and Opportunities: Maintaining Innovation Amidst Fast-Paced Work

While the fast-paced work culture of East Asia has driven significant economic growth and innovation, it also presents challenges. The high pressure to perform quickly can lead to burnout, particularly in industries where long hours are the norm. In countries like Japan and South Korea, the phenomenon of "karoshi" (death from overwork) has sparked discussions about the need for work-life balance and mental health support.

However, the fast-paced work culture also presents opportunities for innovation. Companies in East Asia are leaders in industries such as electronics, automotive, and manufacturing, where speed and efficiency are critical to success. The ability to quickly adapt to new technologies and market trends gives these companies a competitive edge in the global market.

Implications for HR Practices

1. Talent Acquisition and Development

HR practices in East Asia prioritize the recruitment and development of highly skilled and adaptable employees. Organizations invest in comprehensive training programs to equip employees with the skills needed to thrive in a fast-paced environment.

Example: Samsung's extensive employee training programs, including its Global Samsung Leadership Academy, ensure that employees are continuously developing their skills and knowledge to meet the demands of the fast-paced tech industry.

2. Performance Management

Rigorous performance management systems are essential in East Asian work cultures. Regular performance evaluations, clear goal setting, and a focus on measurable outcomes ensure that employees remain aligned with organizational objectives and maintain high productivity levels.

Case Study: At Toyota, performance management includes regular evaluations and feedback sessions, emphasizing continuous improvement and alignment with the company's goals.

3. Work-Life Balance Initiatives

Recognizing the potential downsides of a fast-paced work culture, many East Asian companies are implementing work-life balance initiatives to prevent burnout and enhance employee well-being. Flexible working hours, mental health support, and wellness programs are becoming increasingly common.

Example: In response to the issue of overwork, some Japanese companies have introduced "Premium Fridays," where employees are encouraged to leave work early on the last Friday of the month to promote a healthier work-life balance.

4. Innovation and Creativity

HR practices that foster innovation and creativity are crucial in a fast-paced work culture. Encouraging employees to take risks, experiment with new ideas, and collaborate across departments can drive continuous improvement and maintain a competitive advantage.

"Innovation distinguishes between a leader and a follower." – Steve Jobs.

This mindset is integral to East Asian companies that aim to stay at the forefront of their industries.

HR's Role in Managing the Fast-Paced Work Culture

Human Resources (HR) departments in East Asia play a crucial role in managing the fast-paced work environment. HR professionals must strike a balance between driving efficiency and ensuring employee well-being. This involves implementing policies that promote productivity without sacrificing mental and physical health.

1.Encouraging Continuous Learning:

In fast-paced industries, HR can support employees by offering opportunities for continuous learning and development. Providing training programs that help employees stay up-to-date with the latest technologies and industry trends ensures that they can work efficiently without feeling overwhelmed.

2. Promoting Work-Life Balance:

HR departments must also address the challenges of overwork by promoting work-life balance initiatives. Flexible work hours, mental health programs, and wellness initiatives can help employees manage the pressures of a fast-paced environment.

3. Leveraging Technology for Efficiency:

In East Asia, where technology plays a central role in driving efficiency, HR can implement digital tools and platforms that streamline workflows and reduce manual processes. By leveraging technology, HR can help employees work smarter, not harder, and maintain a high level of productivity.

The fast-paced work culture of East Asia is a powerful driver of efficiency, productivity, and innovation. Rooted in historical developments, Confucian values, and rigorous educational systems, this culture emphasizes hard work, high expectations, and continuous improvement. While the demanding nature of this work environment presents challenges, it also offers significant advantages in terms of organizational performance and competitiveness.

By understanding and leveraging the characteristics of East Asian work culture, HR professionals can implement strategies that enhance productivity, foster innovation, and maintain a motivated and skilled workforce. Balancing the intensity of this culture with initiatives that support employee well-being and work-life balance will be key to sustaining long-term success in the dynamic global market.

The fast-paced work culture of East Asia is deeply rooted in cultural values, childhood education, and societal expectations. From a young age, individuals in countries like Japan, South Korea, and China are taught to value speed, discipline, and efficiency—traits that are essential for success in the modern workplace. While this work culture presents challenges, particularly in terms of work-life balance, it also drives innovation and economic growth. HR professionals in East Asia have the unique task of managing this high-pressure environment while ensuring that employees remain engaged, healthy, and productive.

In summary, the fast-paced work culture in East Asia, with its emphasis on efficiency, productivity, and innovation, offers a model for organizations worldwide seeking to achieve excellence and a competitive advantage. Embracing these cultural traits, while ensuring the well-being of employees, can lead to sustained organizational success and growth.

"Shattering complacency: turning a laid-back mindset into a powerhouse of ambition and unstoppable progress."

CHAPTER 7

Overcoming the Hurdle:

Addressing the Laid-Back Attitude in American Work Culture

American work culture has often been characterized by a relaxed, laid-back attitude, particularly in comparison to the fast-paced, high-pressure environments of East Asia or Europe. This laid-back approach, while fostering creativity and innovation, can sometimes become a hurdle in maintaining consistent productivity and meeting deadlines. Understanding the roots of this attitude—often traced back to childhood experiences and cultural upbringing—can offer insights into how HR professionals can navigate this challenge and foster a more balanced work culture.

The United States has long been seen as a global leader in innovation, technology, and business practices. However, despite its many strengths, certain cultural traits within American work culture can pose significant challenges to organizational progress. One such trait is the tendency toward a laid-back attitude, which, while fostering creativity and work-life balance, can sometimes hinder productivity and long-term growth.

This chapter examines the cultural origins of this attitude, its influence on HR practices, and potential strategies for addressing these challenges to achieve sustained organizational success.

Cultural Roots of the Laid-Back Attitude

1. Historical Context

American work culture has evolved significantly over the centuries. From the industrious spirit of the early settlers and the industrial boom of the 19th and early 20th centuries to the more relaxed and flexible attitudes that emerged in the late 20th and early 21st centuries, the U.S. has seen a broad spectrum of work ethics and attitudes.

2. Emphasis on Individualism and Freedom

American culture places a high value on individualism and personal freedom. This emphasis on autonomy and self-expression can sometimes translate into a more relaxed approach to work, where employees prioritize personal fulfilment and flexibility over rigid productivity metrics.

"The American Dream is that dream of a land in which life should be better and richer and fuller for everyone, with opportunity for each according to ability or achievement." – James Truslow Adams.

This ideal often includes the freedom to balance work with personal interests and leisure.

3. Work-Life Balance

The growing emphasis on work-life balance in the U.S. has led to policies that support flexible working hours, remote work, and ample vacation time. While these policies are beneficial for employee well-being, they can sometimes contribute to a less intense work environment compared to cultures with a more stringent work ethic.

4. Casual Work Environments

The rise of tech companies and startups in Silicon Valley has popularized casual work environments, characterized by relaxed dress codes, flexible schedules, and informal office settings. This shift has influenced broader corporate cultures across the country.

The Childhood Connection to a Laid-Back Attitude

In the United States, childhood experiences often emphasize independence, freedom of choice, and personal responsibility. From a young age, children are encouraged to explore their interests, follow their passions, and make decisions about how they spend their time. This focus on individualism and personal freedom is a hallmark of American culture. While it promotes creativity and self-expression, it can also lead to a more relaxed approach to time management and discipline.

Example: American School Environment

In American schools, there is generally a more flexible approach to structure and discipline compared to other parts of the world. Children are often given the freedom to express their opinions, challenge authority, and work at their own pace. While this encourages creativity and critical thinking, it can also contribute to a more laid-back attitude toward deadlines and punctuality. Group projects and collaborative learning are designed to foster teamwork. Still, the emphasis is often on the process rather than the outcome, which can instill a more relaxed attitude toward completing tasks.

In contrast to countries where strict adherence to schedules is emphasized from an early age (such as Japan or Germany), American children are often encouraged to explore, experiment, and take breaks as needed. This flexibility, while beneficial in fostering innovation, can translate into a more casual approach to work deadlines and productivity in later years.

The Influence of Extracurricular Activities

Another factor contributing to the laid-back attitude in American work culture is the heavy emphasis on extracurricular activities during childhood. Sports, music, and social clubs are often as highly valued as academic performance, and these activities are designed to be fun and enjoyable rather than strictly goal-oriented. The focus on balance between work (school) and play from an early age helps cultivate a mindset that prioritizes overall well-being over rigid schedules.

For example, in American high schools, students often participate in a variety of activities that encourage them to balance multiple commitments at once. However, these activities are rarely driven by strict deadlines, and the primary goal is personal growth and enjoyment, rather than achieving a particular outcome. This can foster a more laid-back attitude toward time management, which may carry over into the workplace.

Laid-Back Attitude in the Workplace

When these children grow up and enter the workforce, the laid-back attitude they've developed during their formative years often translates into a more relaxed approach to work. While American workers are known for their innovation and entrepreneurial spirit, they can face challenges in meeting deadlines, staying focused, and maintaining consistent productivity.

This relaxed attitude can be both a strength and a weakness. On the one hand, it allows for creative problem-solving, flexibility, and adaptability in the workplace. On the other hand, it can lead to procrastination, missed deadlines, and a lack of urgency in high-pressure situations.

Implications of the Laid-Back Attitude on HR Practices

1. Reduced Productivity and Efficiency

A laid-back attitude can sometimes lead to complacency and reduced productivity. Without clear expectations and accountability, employees may struggle to meet deadlines and achieve organizational goals.

Example: A tech start-up with a highly casual culture might experience delays in project delivery due to a lack of structured processes and accountability.

2. Challenges in Performance Management

Implementing effective performance management systems can be challenging in culture that values a laid-back approach to work. Managers may find it difficult to set and enforce high performance standards without being perceived as overly demanding or strict micro-managing.

Case Study: A mid-sized marketing firm in California

struggled with maintaining high performance levels due to its overly relaxed approach to performance evaluations and feedback. The lack of clear metrics and accountability led to inconsistent results and missed growth opportunities.

3. Employee Engagement and Motivation

While a relaxed work environment can enhance job satisfaction and work-life balance, it may also impact employee engagement and motivation. Without a sense of urgency or clear goals, employees might lack the drive to excel and innovate.

Theory: Herzberg's Two-Factor Theory suggests that while hygiene factors (such as a pleasant work environment) prevent dissatisfaction, true motivation stems from factors like achievement, recognition, and responsibility. A laid-back culture might address hygiene factors but fall short on motivators.

4. Innovation and Competitive Edge

A laid-back attitude can hinder innovation and the ability to maintain a competitive edge. In rapidly evolving industries, a more aggressive and proactive approach is often necessary to stay ahead of the competition.

Example: While Google's famous "20% time" policy allows employees to spend a portion of their time on side projects, the company also maintains rigorous standards and expectations to ensure that innovation remains aligned with overall strategic goals.

Strategies to Overcome the Laid-Back Attitude

1. Establishing Clear Goals and Expectations

HR can play a pivotal role in setting clear goals and expectations for employees. By defining specific, measurable, achievable, relevant, and time-bound (SMART) goals, organizations can ensure that employees remain focused and accountable.

Case Study: A financial services firm in New York implemented a structured goal-setting process that included regular check-ins and progress reviews. This approach helped maintain high productivity levels and align individual efforts with the organization's objectives.

2. Balancing Flexibility with Accountability

While maintaining flexibility in work arrangements, HR should also implement systems to ensure accountability. This can include regular performance reviews, transparent metrics, and clear consequences for underperformance.

Example: A software development company introduced flexible work hours but required employees to log their hours and deliverables. This balance allowed for flexibility while ensuring that productivity and accountability were maintained.

3. Enhancing Performance Management Systems

Enhancing performance management systems to incorporate regular feedback, recognition, and development opportunities can help motivate employees and boost performance. HR should focus on creating a culture of continuous improvement and excellence.

"The way to get started is to quit talking and begin doing." – Walt Disney.

Emphasizing action and results over rhetoric can drive a more productive work culture.

4. Fostering a Culture of Innovation and Excellence

Encouraging a culture of innovation and excellence involves recognizing and rewarding innovative ideas and high performance. HR can implement initiatives that celebrate successes, share best practices, and provide platforms for employees to showcase their achievements.

Case Study: At a healthcare technology company, HR introduced an innovation lab where employees could work on new ideas and projects outside of their regular duties. Successful projects were rewarded with bonuses and opportunities for career advancement, fostering a culture of creativity and excellence.

5. Leadership and Role Models

Leaders play a crucial role in shaping organizational culture. HR should ensure that leaders exemplify the desired work ethic and drive for excellence. Providing leadership training and development can help leaders inspire and motivate their teams.

Example: A retail giant's CEO implemented a "lead by example" approach, where executives were expected to demonstrate the same work ethic and commitment they expected from their teams. This approach helped instil a culture of dedication and high performance across the organization.

6. Structured Professional Development Programs

Implementing comprehensive professional development programs can encourage a more proactive approach to work. These programs should focus on skill development, career advancement opportunities, and continuous learning.

Example: A global consulting firm introduced a mandatory professional development program that required employees to complete a specified number of training hours annually. This initiative not only improved employee skills but also fostered a culture of continuous improvement and commitment to excellence.

7. Incentivizing Performance

Creating a robust system of incentives can motivate employees to strive for higher performance levels. This can include financial bonuses, recognition awards, and opportunities for career advancement based on merit.

Case Study: A financial institution implemented a performance-based bonus system that rewarded top performers with significant bonuses and promotions. This approach motivated employees to exceed their targets and contributed to the company's overall success.

8. Creating a Sense of Urgency

Developing a sense of urgency around organizational goals can help counteract a laid-back attitude. This involves setting ambitious yet achievable deadlines, emphasizing the importance of timely results, and creating a culture where speed and efficiency are valued.

Example: An e-commerce company facing intense competition from global players instilled a sense of urgency by setting aggressive growth targets and regularly communicating the importance of quick execution to stay ahead of the competition. This approach helped the company maintain a competitive edge and achieve rapid growth.

HR's Role in Addressing the Laid-Back Attitude

HR professionals in the United States face the unique challenge of balancing the strengths of a laid-back work culture with the need for productivity and accountability. The goal is not to eliminate the laid-back attitude but to channel it in a way that enhances organizational performance.

1. Creating a Balance Between Flexibility and Structure

HR can implement policies that offer flexibility while maintaining accountability. For example, offering flexible work hours or remote work options can cater to employees' desire for freedom, while setting clear expectations and deadlines ensures that productivity remains high.

2. Incorporating Time Management Training

Since many American employees may not have developed strong time management skills during their childhood or educational experiences, HR can offer training programs that help employees manage their time more effectively. By teaching employees how to prioritize tasks and set personal deadlines, HR can help overcome the laid-back attitude that sometimes leads to missed deadlines or procrastination.

3. Encouraging a Results-Oriented Culture

While American culture values the process and personal growth, HR can shift the focus toward results without stifling creativity. Performance-based incentives, clear KPIs, and regular feedback can help employees stay focused on delivering outcomes while maintaining the relaxed work environment that fosters innovation.

4. Emphasizing Work-Life Balance

The laid-back attitude often stems from a desire to maintain a healthy work-life balance. HR can promote policies that support this balance while encouraging productivity during work hours. Offering wellness programs, mental health support, and reasonable workloads can ensure that employees remain motivated and engaged without feeling overwhelmed.

Case Study: The Impact of Flexible Work Policies in a Tech startup

A tech start-up in California struggled with meeting product development deadlines due to its highly relaxed and flexible work environment. Employees were given complete freedom over their schedules, which fostered creativity but led to missed deadlines and inconsistent productivity.

Recognizing this challenge, the HR department introduced a hybrid approach that maintained flexibility while introducing more structured deadlines and accountability measures. Employees were still allowed to set their hours and work remotely, but they were required to provide regular progress updates and meet weekly deadlines.

As a result, the company saw a significant improvement in productivity without sacrificing the creative and laid-back culture that had made it a desirable workplace. By striking the right balance between freedom and accountability, the start-up was able to maintain its innovative edge while enhancing efficiency.

The laid-back attitude in American work culture can be traced back to childhood experiences that emphasize freedom, creativity, and balance. While this relaxed approach fosters innovation and adaptability, it can also pose challenges in maintaining productivity and meeting deadlines. HR professionals play a crucial role in addressing these challenges by fostering a balanced work environment that strikes a balance between flexibility and accountability. By offering time management training, promoting a results-oriented culture, and emphasizing work-life balance, HR can help organizations capitalize on the strengths of a laid-back attitude while mitigating its potential pitfalls.

The laid-back attitude prevalent in some segments of American work culture, while beneficial for creativity and work-life balance, can pose significant challenges to productivity, performance management, and competitive advantage. By understanding the cultural roots of this attitude and its implications, HR professionals can implement strategies to overcome these challenges and drive organizational success.

Balancing flexibility with accountability, enhancing performance management systems, fostering a culture of innovation and excellence, ensuring strong leadership, and implementing structured professional development programs are key strategies for addressing the laid-back attitude in the workplace. By doing so, organizations can harness the strengths of American work culture while mitigating its drawbacks, leading to sustained progress and growth.

In summary, overcoming the laid-back attitude in American work culture requires a proactive and balanced approach. By leveraging effective HR practices and fostering a culture of high performance and innovation, organizations can achieve their goals and maintain a competitive edge in the dynamic global market.

"By conquering cultural challenges, Africa unlocks its true potential, paving the way for progress and prosperity."

CHAPTER 8

Overcoming Cultural Challenges for Progress in Africa

Africa, a continent rich in natural resources and cultural diversity, has faced numerous challenges in its path toward development. Each region in Africa presents unique opportunities and challenges for growth and development. Among these challenges is the cultural approach often characterized by a laid-back attitude, sometimes interpreted as "let it go easy," and a different perception of time compared to Western standards.

While Africa is often recognized for its vast natural resources and emerging economies, progress in many areas is hindered by cultural challenges deeply rooted in the early experiences of its people.

This chapter examines how childhood experiences and cultural influences in various African countries shape work behaviors, and how HR professionals can navigate these challenges to drive organizational progress. It also explores how Human Resources (HR) can work differently to overcome these cultural challenges and assesses the potential for progress across the African continent.

Childhood Experiences and Cultural Foundations

In many African societies, the role of the family and community is central to a child's upbringing. Children are often raised in close-knit communities where collective responsibility is emphasized over individual achievement. While this fosters a strong sense of belonging and community, it can also create challenges when it comes to promoting individual ambition and driving personal progress.

Example: Communal Upbringing in African Villages

In rural areas across Africa, children grow up in environments where communal living and shared responsibilities are the norm. From a young age, children are taught to contribute to the well-being of the community by helping with household chores, farming, or caring for younger siblings. While this promotes teamwork and a sense of unity, it can also instill a mindset where individual goals are secondary to the collective good.

This communal upbringing, while beneficial in maintaining strong community ties, can sometimes clash with the competitive nature of modern workplaces, where individual performance and ambition are often rewarded. HR professionals working in African organizations must navigate this tension by finding ways to encourage personal initiative without undermining the collective values that are so deeply ingrained in the culture.

Educational Challenges and Access to Resources

Access to quality education is a significant challenge in many African countries, particularly in rural areas. For many children, the early years of education are marked by a lack of resources, overcrowded classrooms, and undertrained teachers. This early exposure to educational challenges can have long-term effects on work habits and attitudes toward progress.

In countries such as Kenya and Nigeria, children often walk long distances to school, attend classes in poorly equipped facilities, and face difficulties accessing books and other learning materials. These challenges can instill resilience and resourcefulness, but they can also create gaps in foundational skills, such as time management and critical thinking, that are essential for success in the modern workplace.

Cultural Perceptions of Authority and Leadership

In many African cultures, respect for authority is deeply ingrained, beginning in childhood with deference to elders. Children are taught to respect and follow the guidance of older family members, teachers, and community leaders. While this respect for authority helps maintain social order, it can sometimes stifle creativity and innovation, as individuals may be reluctant to challenge authority or propose new ideas.

In the workplace, this cultural trait can create challenges for organizations that seek to foster innovation and encourage employees to think critically or propose new solutions. HR professionals must strike a balance between respecting cultural norms and promoting a more dynamic and open work environment where employees feel empowered to contribute their ideas.

Case Study: Leadership Styles in South African Corporations

In South Africa, businesses are increasingly embracing more egalitarian leadership styles that encourage open communication and collaboration. However, for many employees raised in traditional African households, this shift can be difficult to navigate. Employees may be hesitant to speak up in meetings or challenge the opinions of senior leaders, as doing so goes against their cultural upbringing.

To address this, HR professionals in South Africa have implemented leadership development programs that teach employees how to balance respect for authority with the need for innovation and critical thinking. By providing training that encourages open dialogue and respectful dissent, companies have seen improvements in employee engagement and innovation.

The Cultural Landscape

Africa's cultural diversity is immense, comprising over 3,000 ethnic groups and numerous languages, traditions, and belief systems. This diversity brings a richness that is unparalleled but also presents challenges in terms of establishing uniform practices that can drive development. One cultural trait often noted is the relaxed approach to time and deadlines, commonly referred to as "African time." This concept reflects a more flexible and less rigid approach to time management compared to the more punctual Western cultures.

Understanding "Let it Go Easy" and "African Time"

"Let it Go Easy": This cultural approach reflects a preference for maintaining harmony and avoiding confrontation when dealing with issues. It emphasizes a relaxed, patient, and non-aggressive way of resolving challenges, creating an environment where relationships and interpersonal dynamics are prioritized over rigid rules or deadlines. While this promotes peace and reduces unnecessary conflict, it can sometimes result in delays or a lack of urgency when addressing pressing problems or capitalizing on new opportunities. This mindset, while valuable for fostering harmony, requires careful management to ensure that it does not hinder progress or efficiency.

"African Time": This concept represents a cultural orientation in which events, tasks, and commitments are approached with a flexible sense of time. Rather than adhering strictly to schedules or deadlines, actions take place when individuals are ready and circumstances align. This creates a more fluid, adaptable, and less predictable approach to planning and execution. While it allows for spontaneity and responsiveness to immediate needs, it can sometimes challenge productivity and efficiency in environments that require precise timing and structured processes.

Both of these cultural traits, though sometimes viewed as obstacles to productivity, are deeply ingrained in the social fabric of many communities. They are not merely habits but reflections of values such as community, adaptability, and relationship-building. As such, they cannot simply be dismissed or drastically altered. Instead, they must be understood in context and integrated into broader strategies that respect cultural nuances while driving progress. By balancing these cultural approaches with structured planning and clear objectives, organizations can harness their strengths while mitigating potential downsides, fostering both harmony and development.

HR Strategies to Overcome Cultural Challenges

Human Resources (HR) departments play a critical role in navigating and bridging cultural differences to foster development. Here are some strategies HR can employ to address the laid-back cultural approach and different perceptions of time:

1. Cultural Sensitivity Training:

HR can organize training sessions that educate employees about the importance of time management and the benefits of a more structured approach to work. These sessions should be sensitive to cultural norms and seek to find a balance rather than imposing foreign practices.

2. Incentivizing Punctuality and Efficiency:

Introducing incentives for the timely completion of tasks and adherence to schedules can motivate employees to adopt more efficient work habits. Rewards can be tailored to align with cultural values, making them more appealing and effective.

3. Flexible yet Structured Schedules:

Developing a hybrid scheduling system that combines flexibility with structure can help. For example, allowing for flexible start times but setting firm deadlines for task completion can accommodate cultural preferences while maintaining productivity.

4. Clear Communication and Expectations:

HR should ensure that goals, expectations, and deadlines are communicated clearly and consistently. Providing regular feedback and creating open channels of communication can help address any misunderstandings or delays promptly.

5. Local Leadership Development:

Investing in the development of local leaders who understand the cultural context and can act as change agents is crucial. These leaders can bridge the gap between traditional practices and modern business requirements.

6. Community Engagement:

Engaging with local communities and understanding their needs and values can help in designing HR policies that are more culturally relevant and accepted.

Case Studies and Examples

Case Study 1: Unilever in Africa

Unilever, a global consumer goods company, has successfully adapted its HR strategies to fit the African context. Recognizing the importance of local culture, Unilever invested in leadership development programs for local managers. These programs included cultural sensitivity training and workshops on time management, emphasizing the importance of balancing cultural practices with business needs. By empowering local leaders and fostering a deep understanding of the local context, Unilever has improved productivity and maintained harmonious workplace relationships.

Case Study 2: Safaricom in Kenya

Safaricom, Kenya's leading telecommunications company, faced challenges related to "African time" in its operations. To address this, the HR department implemented a flexible scheduling system that allowed employees to choose their start and end times within a set framework. This flexibility was combined with clear deadlines and performance metrics. Additionally, Safaricom introduced a rewards program that recognized and incentivized timely completion of projects. This approach helped align the cultural preference for flexibility with the company's productivity goals, leading to increased efficiency and employee satisfaction.

Will Africa Rise?

The question of whether Africa will rise is both complex and multifaceted, with numerous factors influencing the continent's trajectory. Africa has already demonstrated significant potential and growth in various sectors, including technology, finance, and natural resources. Countries such as Kenya, Nigeria, and South Africa have become hubs for innovation, attracting significant investments and driving economic growth. However, progress has been uneven, with some nations experiencing more rapid growth than others. Persistent challenges, such as political instability, corruption, and inadequate infrastructure, continue to impede the continent's development and hinder its full potential.

The cultural traits of "let it go easy" and "African time" should not be viewed as insurmountable obstacles. Instead, they are part of a rich cultural heritage that can be leveraged positively in the pursuit of progress. These cultural values emphasize flexibility, relationship-building, and patience—traits that can be powerful tools when integrated into a business or organizational strategy. By adopting innovative HR strategies that take these cultural nuances into account and fostering a deeper understanding of local contexts, businesses can create environments where these cultural traits contribute to success, rather than limit it.

Ultimately, Africa's rise will depend on a delicate balance of internal reforms, external support, and the ability to adapt global best practices to the unique needs of local communities. With the right approach, Africa can harness its vast potential, overcome existing challenges, and achieve sustainable development. As more attention is devoted to building strong institutions, improving infrastructure, and investing in human capital, the continent is poised to continue its upward trajectory and make significant contributions to the global economy.

Overcoming the Cultural Hurdle for Progress

For Africa to progress, both economically and socially, it is essential to address the cultural challenges that stem from early childhood experiences. HR professionals play a crucial role in overcoming these hurdles by developing strategies that align with African values while promoting growth and innovation.

1. Encouraging Personal Initiative While Respecting Community Values

HR professionals must find ways to encourage individual ambition and personal initiative without undermining the importance of community. This can be achieved by implementing recognition programs that reward both individual and team achievements, creating a balanced approach to performance management.

2. Providing Access to Continuous Learning and Development

Given the educational challenges many employees face in their formative years, HR departments should prioritize continuous learning and development opportunities. By offering training programs, mentorship, and skills development initiatives, organizations can help bridge the gap in foundational skills and equip employees with the necessary tools to succeed in a competitive global market.

3. Fostering a Culture of Open Communication and Innovation

To overcome the cultural challenges related to respect for authority, HR must create a work environment where open communication is encouraged and valued. Leadership training programs that focus on collaborative leadership styles can help employees feel more comfortable expressing their ideas and contributing to the organization's success.

The cultural challenges that arise from childhood experiences in Africa are both unique and deeply rooted in the continent's traditions and values. While these challenges can hinder progress, they also present opportunities for HR professionals to create strategies that align with African culture while fostering growth, innovation, and development. By understanding the cultural foundations that shape work behaviour and addressing the barriers to progress, HR can play a pivotal role in driving Africa's continued advancement.

In conclusion, Africa's cultural approach to time and work presents unique challenges and opportunities. By embracing these cultural traits and strategically integrating them into HR practices, the continent can make significant strides toward progress and prosperity. Through effective leadership, cultural sensitivity, and strategic planning, Africa can harness its rich cultural heritage to drive development and achieve long-term success.

"Balancing fairness and recognition, HR faces the challenge of using appraisal systems to truly satisfy and motivate employees."

CHAPTER 9

HR Challenges in Satisfying Employees Through Appraisal Systems

Human Resources (HR) departments face significant challenges in designing and implementing performance appraisal systems that meet the needs of employees across diverse cultural contexts and organizational structures. The process of appraising employee performance is complex, involving various stakeholders, cultural nuances, and evolving workplace expectations.

This chapter delves into the difficulties HR encounters in satisfying employees, the different types of appraisal systems used globally, how different continents and countries adopt and adapt these systems, and strategies to overcome these challenges. Case studies and examples are provided to illustrate these points.

HR Challenges in Satisfying Employees:

Cultural Differences: Employees from diverse cultural backgrounds have varying expectations regarding feedback, recognition, and career progression. For example, while direct feedback might be appreciated in some cultures, it can be perceived as confrontational in others. HR must navigate these cultural sensitivities to ensure the appraisal process is respectful and effective.

Communication Barriers: Clear communication is critical for effective performance appraisals. However, language differences, indirect communication styles, and varying levels of understanding can impede the appraisal process, leading to misunderstandings and dissatisfaction among employees.

Bias and Fairness: Ensuring that appraisals are fair and unbiased is a significant challenge. Managers may inadvertently bring personal biases into the appraisal process, which can affect the objectivity and fairness of performance evaluations. This can lead to feelings of inequity and resentment among employees.

Alignment with Organizational Goals: Performance appraisal systems must align with the organization's goals and values. However, ensuring that individual performance metrics contribute to broader organizational objectives while also being relevant and motivating for employees can be difficult.

Evolving Expectations: The modern workforce has increasingly evolving expectations, including a desire for continuous feedback, career development opportunities, and a healthy work-life balance. Traditional appraisal systems may not meet these needs, leading to dissatisfaction.

Technology Integration: The integration of technology into appraisal systems can streamline the process and provide valuable data insights. However, it also introduces challenges such as ensuring data privacy, managing technological changes, and addressing employees' concerns about being constantly monitored.

Case Studies and Examples:

Case Study 1: Google's OKRs (Objectives and Key Results)

Google utilizes the OKR framework to establish and assess performance goals. This system involves setting ambitious, measurable goals (Objectives) and defining specific results (Key Results) to track progress. OKRs are transparent across the organization, allowing employees to see how their work aligns with the company's goals. Regular check-ins and updates promote continuous feedback and adjustment. This approach has helped Google balance global consistency with local relevance while fostering a culture of innovation and accountability.

Case Study 2 : Adobe's Check-in System

Adobe replaced its traditional annual review process with a more flexible and continuous check-in system. Managers and employees have regular, informal conversations about performance, goals, and development needs. This system eliminates the stress of annual reviews and provides timely feedback, enabling employees to make real-time improvements. Adobe's approach has led to increased employee engagement, satisfaction, and retention.

Example : Siemens' Balanced Scorecard Approach

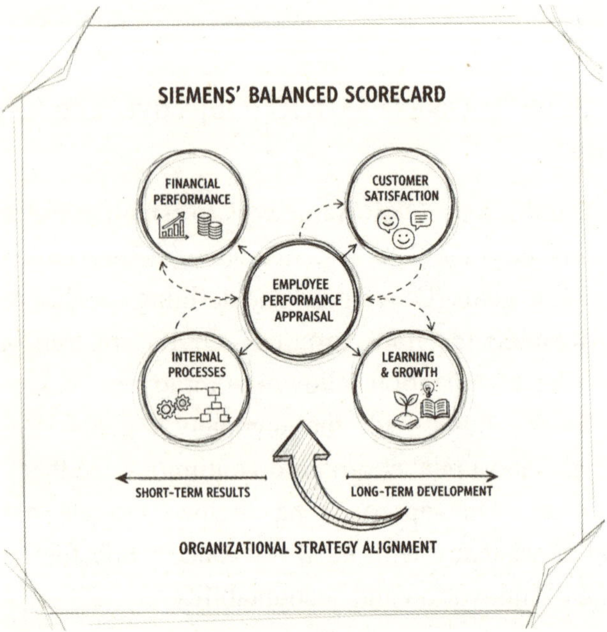

Siemens uses a Balanced Scorecard approach to performance appraisals, integrating financial and non-financial performance metrics. This system evaluates employees based on multiple perspectives, including financial performance, customer satisfaction, internal processes, and learning and growth. By balancing short-term results with long-term development, Siemens ensures a holistic assessment of employee performance, aligned with organizational strategy.

Different Types of Appraisal Systems

Traditional Performance Appraisals:

Annual Reviews: These are formal, structured appraisals that occur once a year. They involve evaluating an employee's performance against predefined criteria, setting goals for the upcoming year, and discussing career development opportunities. While thorough, annual reviews can be perceived as infrequent and reactive, meaning that employees only receive feedback once a year rather than in real time. This can delay improvements and make it harder to address issues promptly.

Rating Scales: This method involves rating employees on a scale (e.g., 1-5) across various performance dimensions, such as communication, leadership, and problem-solving skills. It's easy to administer and provides a straightforward way to compare employees. However, it can be overly simplistic and may be influenced by rating biases, such as leniency, central tendency, or halo effects, which can affect the accuracy and fairness of the assessment.

Modern Performance Appraisals:

360 Degree Feedback: This system gathers feedback from a variety of sources, including peers, subordinates, supervisors, and sometimes even customers. The feedback provides a comprehensive view of an employee's performance and behavior, allowing for a more balanced and holistic assessment. However, this method can be time-consuming and challenging to manage, particularly when it comes to collecting, analyzing, and acting on the feedback provided by multiple sources.

Continuous Feedback: Instead of waiting for annual reviews, employees receive ongoing feedback throughout the year. This system encourages continuous improvement, fosters timely recognition, and allows managers to address issues as they arise. However, it requires a significant cultural shift within the organization and a strong commitment from managers to provide consistent and constructive feedback.

Objective-Based Appraisals:

Management by Objectives (MBO): MBO involves setting specific, measurable goals at the beginning of the appraisal period. Employees and managers collaborate to define objectives that align with the company's strategic goals, and performance is evaluated based on the achievement of these goals. While this method helps to align individual performance with organizational goals, it can be rigid and overly focused on short-term results, potentially neglecting the broader context of long-term development and growth.

Key Performance Indicators (KPIs): Employees are evaluated based on their performance against specific, quantifiable metrics such as sales targets, production quotas, or customer satisfaction scores. This system is data-driven and objective, making it easier to assess performance accurately. However, it may overlook important qualitative aspects of performance, such as teamwork, creativity, and problem-solving, which can be harder to measure.

Development Appraisals:

Behaviourally Anchored Rating Scales (BARS): BARS combines both quantitative and qualitative data by describing specific behaviours for different performance levels. This method provides clear examples of what constitutes different performance standards, reducing ambiguity and enhancing objectivity in the evaluation. However, it can be complex to develop and may require significant resources to create detailed descriptions of behaviours for each performance level.

Personal Development Plans (PDPs): PDPs are focused on the long-term growth and development of employees. They involve setting personal development goals, identifying resources, and offering support to help employees achieve those goals. This approach encourages continuous learning and career development. However, it requires ongoing commitment and follow-through from both employees and managers to ensure progress is made and goals are achieved.

Each of these appraisal systems has its own strengths and limitations, and organizations may need to tailor their approach depending on their specific needs, culture, and objectives. A combination of different appraisal methods can often provide a more balanced and effective assessment of employee performance and potential.

Adoption and Adaptation of Appraisal Systems Across Continents:

North America :

United States: The U.S. is known for its structured and goal-oriented appraisal systems, such as MBO and KPIs. Employees generally accept direct feedback and individual performance evaluations, as these align with the culture of individualism and meritocracy. Continuous feedback mechanisms are increasingly popular, reflecting the value placed on innovation and agility.

Canada : Similar to U.S., Canadian organizations use structured appraisals, with an added focus on employee well-being and work-life balance. Employees appreciate clear, direct communication, but there is a strong emphasis on inclusivity and fairness in the appraisal process.

Europe :

United Kingdom : The UK employs formal appraisal systems like annual reviews and 360-degree feedback. British employees generally accept structured feedback but also value a conversational approach. The emphasis on professionalism and transparency helps in maintaining satisfaction.

Germany : German companies emphasize precision and thoroughness in their appraisal. Employees expect detailed, objective evaluations and value the clarity and predictability of performance metrics. The cultural appreciation for efficiency and structure supports the acceptance of formal appraisal systems.

France : In France, appraisals tend to be more informal and conversational. Employees appreciate open dialogue and constructive feedback, aligning with the cultural emphasis on personal relationships and work-life balance.

Asia :

Japan : Japanese companies often use a mix of seniority-based and performance-based appraisal. Employees value group harmony and long-term employment, so appraisal focuses on team performance and incremental development. Direct feedback is less common, and feedback is often delivered indirectly to maintain harmony.

China : In China, performance appraisals are increasingly adopting Western practices, but guanxi (relationships) and respect for hierarchy remain important. Employees accept performance-based metrics but expect feedback to be respectful and considerate of social hierarchies.

India : Indian companies are blending traditional hierarchical practices with modern appraisal systems like continuous feedback and KPIs. Employees expect respect for seniority and appreciate clear, supportive feedback that considers personal development and growth opportunities.

Africa :

South Africa : South African companies use a blend of Western practices and local cultural nuances. Performance appraisals are structured but also focus on inclusivity and diversity. Employees appreciate open communication and empowerment, reflecting the cultural emphasis on community and equality.

Nigeria : In Nigeria, appraisals are often less formal, focusing on achieving results and personal relationships. Employees expect respect for hierarchy and clear recognition of their efforts. Feedback is generally well-received if delivered respectfully and constructively.

South America :

Brazil : Brazilian companies often use a mix of formal appraisals and informal feedback. Employees value personal relationships and open communication, aligning with the cultural emphasis on social connection and well-being. Appraisals that incorporate these elements are more likely to be accepted.

Argentina: In Argentina, performance appraisals are formal yet flexible, with a focus on achieving business goals and fostering good interpersonal relationships. Employees appreciate a balanced approach that considers both professional achievements and personal satisfaction.

HR department faces significant challenges in designing and implementing performance appraisal systems that satisfy employees across diverse cultural and organizational contexts. By understanding and addressing cultural differences, enhancing communication, mitigating biases, aligning appraisals with organizational goals, responding to evolving employee expectations, and effectively integrating technology, HR can overcome these challenges. Case studies of companies like Google, Adobe, and Siemens demonstrate how innovative and adaptable appraisal systems can lead to increased employee satisfaction, engagement, and organizational success. Through thoughtful design and strategic implementation, HR can create appraisal systems that not only evaluate performance but also drive growth and development for both employees and the organization.

"India's rich cultural diversity challenges HR to build inclusive strategies that unite, empower, and drive excellence across its dynamic landscape."

CHAPTER 10

India - A Country Within a Country:

Navigating Cultural Diversity in HR Management

India, with its vast geographical expanse and a population exceeding 1.4 billion, is a tapestry of diverse cultures, languages, traditions, and social norms. This diversity makes India a unique environment for Human Resources (HR) management, where cultural nuances significantly influence human behaviour, habits, work culture, and organizational systems.

This chapter examines the complexities of managing cultural differences in India, the strategies HR professionals employ to address these differences, and the implications for organizational success. We will also delve into the state-wise differences across various regions of India, which is divided into North, South, East, West, and Central, and understand how these differences impact HR practices.

Understanding India's Cultural Diversity

India's diversity is unparalleled, with over 2,000 distinct ethnic groups, 22 officially recognized languages, and hundreds of dialects. This diversity extends to various aspects of life, including:

1. Regional Variations Each state in India has its own distinct culture, language, cuisine, and traditions. For example, the work culture in metropolitan cities like Mumbai and Delhi differs significantly from that in smaller towns or rural areas.

2. Religious Diversity India is home to major world religions, including Hinduism, Islam, Christianity, Sikhism, Buddhism, and Jainism. Each religion brings its own unique set of cultural practices and festivals, which can impact workplace dynamics and employee needs.

3. Socio-Economic Differences The socio-economic landscape in India is varied, with significant disparities between urban and rural areas. This influences access to education, technology, and opportunities, affecting workforce composition and expectations.

Human Behaviour and Habits

Human behaviour and habits in India are shaped by its rich cultural heritage and societal norms. Key characteristics include:

1. Collectivism vs. Individualism

Indian society leans towards collectivism, where family and community play a central role in an individual's life. This contrasts with Western individualism and impacts workplace dynamics, emphasizing teamwork and group harmony over individual achievement.

2. Respect for Hierarchy:

Indian culture places a high value on hierarchy and respect for authority. This is reflected in organizational structures, where employees may be less likely to challenge superiors openly and prefer a top-down approach to decision-making.

3. Interpersonal Relationships:

Building personal relationships is crucial in India. Trust and rapport often precede business transactions and collaborations. Networking and informal interactions can play a significant role in career advancement and workplace harmony.

Cultural Influences on Work Culture

Work culture in India is shaped by a combination of cultural, social, and economic factors, creating a unique environment that blends traditional values with modern work practices. These influences significantly impact how individuals approach their roles, interact with colleagues, and adapt to organizational goals. Below are some key cultural aspects that shape the Indian workplace:

Work Ethic:

Indian professionals are widely recognized for their dedication, perseverance, and strong work ethic.

Historically, there has been a deep-rooted respect for hard work, often influenced by cultural and familial values. Employees take pride in their contributions and are willing to go the extra mile to meet organizational goals. However, with the rise of a younger, more progressive generation, the concept of work-life balance has gained significant traction. Younger professionals are increasingly prioritizing personal well-being, leisure, and family time alongside their careers, pushing organizations to adopt policies that support flexibility and holistic well-being.

Flexibility and Adaptability:

Indian employees are often noted for their exceptional flexibility and adaptability in the workplace. This stems from the diverse and dynamic socio-economic conditions prevalent in the country, where changes in technology, markets, and organizational priorities are frequent. Employees are accustomed to navigating uncertainty and adapting to varying circumstances, whether it involves working with global teams, embracing new technologies, or managing unexpected challenges. This adaptability has made Indian professionals highly sought after in global markets, as they can seamlessly integrate into diverse work environments and drive success in dynamic scenarios.

Communication Styles:

Communication in India is often characterized by subtlety, nuance, and an emphasis on relationships. Unlike direct communication styles seen in some Western cultures,

Indian communication tends to be indirect, with non-verbal cues, context, and interpersonal dynamics playing a crucial role in conveying messages. For example, employees may hesitate to give direct criticism or may prioritize maintaining harmony over confrontation. This nuanced approach to communication can be challenging for outsiders to interpret but is deeply rooted in the cultural values of respect and relationship-building. For HR professionals and managers, understanding these subtleties is essential to fostering effective communication, ensuring clarity, and building trust within teams.

In summary, India's work culture is a reflection of its rich and diverse heritage, blending traditional values with the demands of a modern, globalized economy. Organizations that understand and embrace these cultural influences can create environments that maximize employee engagement, enhance productivity, and foster innovation while respecting the unique characteristics of their workforce.

State-wise Differences Across Regions

1. North India

States: Delhi, Punjab, Haryana, Uttar Pradesh, Himachal Pradesh, Uttarakhand, Rajasthan.

Cultural Traits: North Indians generally have a more direct communication style and are known for their hospitality. There is a strong emphasis on family and community ties.

Work Culture: The work culture in North India, especially in Delhi and NCR, is fast-paced and competitive. There is a strong hierarchical structure in organizations, and respect for authority is paramount. Employees often value stability and job security.

HR Practices: HR policies often emphasize structured career progression and formal recognition programs. Employee engagement activities frequently include community and family-oriented events.

2. South India

States: Karnataka, Tamil Nadu, Kerala, Andhra Pradesh, Telangana.

Cultural Traits: South Indians are known for their discipline, education focus, and respect for tradition. There is a high value placed on education and professional qualifications.

Work Culture: The work culture in South India, particularly in cities like Bengaluru and Hyderabad, is known for its emphasis on technology and innovation. There is a collaborative work environment, and a significant focus is placed on professional development.

HR Practices: HR strategies in South India often include continuous learning opportunities, professional development programs, and inclusive decision-making processes. Employee wellness and work-life balance are also key focus areas.

3. East India

States: West Bengal, Odisha, Bihar, Jharkhand, Assam, other north-eastern states.

Cultural Traits: East Indians are known for their intellectualism, artistic inclinations, and strong cultural heritage. There is a rich tradition of literature, music, and art.

Work Culture: The work culture in East India varies, with Kolkata being a major business hub known for its intellectual workforce. There is a balance between professional responsibilities and cultural pursuits.

HR Practices: HR policies in East India often emphasize creativity, innovation, and cultural engagement. Employee engagement activities may include cultural events, artistic performances, and intellectual discussions.

4. West India

States: Maharashtra, Gujarat, Goa.

Cultural Traits: West Indians are known for their entrepreneurial spirit, business acumen, and cosmopolitan outlook. Mumbai, as the financial capital, is a melting pot of diverse cultures.

Work Culture: The work culture in West India, especially in cities like Mumbai and Pune, is highly dynamic, competitive, and fast-paced. There is a strong emphasis on professional achievements and career growth.

HR Practices: HR strategies in West India often include performance-based incentives, career development programs, and a focus on diversity and inclusion. Networking and professional connections are highly valued.

5. Central India

States: Madhya Pradesh, Chhattisgarh.

Cultural Traits: Central Indians are known for their traditional values, hospitality, and simplicity. There is a strong connection to the land and agricultural practices.

Work Culture: The work culture in Central India is often community-oriented and less formal. There is a strong emphasis on mutual respect and collaboration.

HR Practices: HR policies in Central India focus on community engagement, agricultural support initiatives, and skill development programs. There is a significant focus on employee well-being and local economic development.

Language Barriers in HR Across States

One of the most significant challenges HR professionals face when managing a culturally diverse workforce in India is language. With 22 officially recognized languages and hundreds of regional dialects, communication within organizations can become a barrier to effective collaboration. When employees from different states, such as Tamil Nadu, Gujarat, and West Bengal, come together in the workplace, they may struggle to understand one another, even if they share a common language like English or Hindi.

For HR professionals, addressing these language barriers is critical to fostering a cohesive work environment. Training sessions, team meetings, and even day-to-day communication can be hindered if employees do not share a comfortable working language. HR departments often need to implement strategies to bridge these language gaps, such as:

- Multilingual Training Materials: Providing training in multiple languages or offering translation services to ensure that employees from different linguistic backgrounds can fully engage with the content.

- Language Support: Offering language classes or creating language buddy systems where employees help one another navigate language challenges.

- Clear and Simplified Communication: Ensuring that internal communication is clear and simplified, avoiding jargon or complex language that might confuse employees who are not native speakers.

Example: Language Challenges in IT Hubs

In cities like Bengaluru and Hyderabad, where employees from all over India come to work in the tech industry, language differences can create confusion, especially when employees default to their native languages in informal settings. HR teams often encourage the use of English as a neutral language for official communication, while fostering a culture of inclusivity where regional languages are respected and supported in informal interactions.

Differences in Food Habits and the HR Challenge

Another cultural aspect that plays a significant role in Indian workplaces is food. India's diverse regions have their own distinct cuisines, food habits, and dietary restrictions, which can sometimes create tension or discomfort in shared workspaces. Employees from North India may have different food preferences than those from South India, and this diversity can pose challenges in communal spaces like cafeterias or during work events.

For example, in a workplace where employees from Gujarat, a state with a largely vegetarian population, work alongside employees from Kerala, who may prefer non-vegetarian meals, HR professionals must be sensitive to these preferences. Ensuring that everyone feels comfortable and respected in shared dining spaces is important for maintaining harmony.

Example: Navigating Dietary Differences in Corporate Events

HR departments often face challenges when organizing corporate events or team lunches, where catering to everyone's food preferences is essential. A company that hosts a team lunch in a largely vegetarian office may need to ensure that there are sufficient non-vegetarian options for employees from other regions, and vice versa. Similarly, understanding the religious or cultural dietary restrictions, such as avoiding beef or pork, is crucial in planning inclusive meals.

To address these challenges, HR teams can:

• Offer Diverse Meal Options: Ensure that cafeterias and catering services provide a variety of meal options, including vegetarian, non-vegetarian, and culturally appropriate dishes.

• Foster Open Communication: Encourage employees to openly express their food preferences or restrictions, enabling HR to create an inclusive environment.

• Promote Cultural Food Exchanges: Organize events where employees can share their regional foods, fostering a sense of cultural exchange and appreciation in the workplace.

HR Strategies for Managing Cultural Differences

1. Cultural Sensitivity Training

HR departments conduct cultural sensitivity training to help employees understand and respect diverse cultural backgrounds. This training covers communication styles, social norms, and the importance of inclusivity.

2. Flexible Policies

HR policies are designed to be flexible and inclusive, accommodating various cultural practices and religious observances. For example, leave policies may consider regional festivals and religious holidays.

3. Localized Management Practices

Organizations adapt their management practices to suit regional preferences and cultural norms. For instance, team-building activities and motivational strategies may vary between regions to align with local values and behaviors.

4. Promoting Inclusivity:

HR initiatives focus on promoting inclusivity and diversity within the workplace. This includes creating platforms for diverse voices to be heard and addressing biases in recruitment, appraisals, and promotions.

5. Employee Engagement Programs:

Regular employee engagement programs are conducted to foster a sense of belonging and community. These programs often include cultural celebrations, team outings, and interactive workshops.

Case Studies and Examples

Case Study 1: Infosys

Infosys, one of India's leading IT companies, has implemented various strategies to manage cultural diversity. The company conducts regular cultural sensitivity workshops and promotes an inclusive work environment. Infosys celebrates regional festivals and encourages employees to share their cultural traditions, fostering mutual respect and understanding.

Case Study 2: Tata Group

The Tata Group, with its diverse portfolio of companies, has a robust HR framework that respects cultural diversity. Tata's HR policies are designed to be inclusive, with specific initiatives to support gender diversity, regional inclusivity, and employee well-being. The group's emphasis on ethics and community service aligns with Indian cultural values of collectivism and social responsibility.

Example: Microsoft India

Microsoft India has embraced flexible work policies to cater to the diverse needs of its workforce. The company offers flexible working hours, work-from-home options, and comprehensive wellness programs. Microsoft India's approach recognizes the importance of work-life balance and the varied cultural expectations of its employees.

Managing cultural diversity in India requires a nuanced understanding of the country's rich tapestry of cultures, languages, and traditions. HR departments play a crucial role in fostering an inclusive and respectful work environment that accommodates these differences. By implementing strategies such as cultural sensitivity training, flexible policies, localized management practices, and promoting inclusivity, HR can effectively navigate the complexities of India's diverse workforce. Successful case studies from companies like Infosys, Tata Group, and Microsoft India demonstrate that embracing cultural diversity can lead to a more harmonious and productive workplace, ultimately contributing to organizational success.

The diversity of language and food habits in India adds to the complexity of managing a culturally diverse workforce. HR professionals must navigate these differences carefully to create a harmonious work environment where employees from different states feel included and respected. By addressing language barriers and accommodating diverse food preferences, organizations can foster a more inclusive and culturally sensitive workplace, ultimately contributing to employee satisfaction and productivity.

"Success lies in reshaping global HR strategies to align with the unique pulse of local realities."

CHAPTER 11

The Regional HR Practice :

Adapting Global Strategies to Local Realities

In today's globalized world, organizations are increasingly adopting standardized HR strategies that align with international best practices. However, the success of these strategies largely depends on their ability to adapt to regional nuances. Regional HR practices vary greatly due to differences in cultural values, labour laws, and social expectations, making it essential for global companies to tailor their HR policies to local realities.

Today, we can say the world is interconnected, organizations operate across borders and cultures, making the role of human resources (HR) more complex than ever before. A one-size-fits-all approach no longer works; regional practices need to be integrated into global strategies to align with diverse cultural, social, and legal landscapes.

This chapter examines the variations in regional HR practices worldwide and how businesses can tailor their global HR strategies to succeed in diverse cultural contexts. It also explores how organizations navigate these regional differences, providing examples of how global HR strategies are adapted to meet local needs.

The Importance of Regional HR Practices

Cultural diversity is far more than just differences in language, traditions, or customs; it profoundly influences how individuals approach work, interact with colleagues, and respond to leadership. It shapes the way people collaborate, perceive authority, and find motivation in their professional lives. For organizations aiming to succeed in an increasingly interconnected and globalized world, recognizing and embracing these regional differences is not just beneficial—it is essential.

Consider a multinational company with its headquarters in the United States and offices in India, China, and Brazil. Each of these regions has its own unique cultural dynamics that require tailored HR strategies to ensure success. For example, leadership styles may need to be adapted to resonate with local expectations—employees in one region might thrive under a participative leadership approach, while those in another may prefer a more hierarchical structure. Communication norms can also vary significantly, with some cultures valuing direct, straightforward exchanges and others relying heavily on context and non-verbal cues to convey meaning.

Work-life balance expectations are another critical factor that can differ across regions. In some countries, employees may prioritize flexibility and personal time, while in others, long hours and dedication to the job are seen as a badge of honour. Similarly, different factors can drive employee motivation—some cultures may value individual recognition and financial rewards, while others might prioritize teamwork, job security, or opportunities for personal growth.

By investing in a deep understanding of these cultural nuances and implementing region-specific HR practices, companies can create work environments that respect and leverage these differences. This localized approach helps foster a more engaged, motivated, and productive workforce while also ensuring alignment with the organization's broader goals. Furthermore, it enables businesses to build stronger relationships with employees, reduce turnover, and create a sense of belonging across diverse teams.

In conclusion, the importance of regional HR practices cannot be overstated in today's global business landscape. Organizations that take the time to understand and integrate local cultural values into their HR strategies are better positioned to thrive, driving both employee satisfaction and overall success.

Key Aspects of Regional HR Variations

1. Leadership and Hierarchy

In Western countries, particularly in the U.S. and parts of Europe, leadership tends to be more participatory and collaborative. Employees often expect to be included in decision-making processes and may feel empowered to express their opinions freely. In contrast, countries in Asia and the Middle East may follow a more hierarchical structure, where decisions are made at the top, and respect for authority is deeply ingrained.

To manage this difference, HR professionals need to develop leadership programs that align with the cultural expectations of each region. A leadership style that works well in New York may not be as effective in Tokyo, where a more reserved and hierarchical approach may be required.

2. Communication Styles

Communication is another area where regional differences are profound. In cultures such as Germany or Switzerland, direct and precise communication is valued. Employees expect clear guidelines and direct feedback. However, in countries like Japan or India, communication tends to be more indirect. Employees may be less likely to voice disagreement or concerns openly due to cultural norms of preserving harmony.

For HR, this means developing communication policies that respect these cultural nuances. Feedback mechanisms, team meetings, and even day-to-day conversations must be adapted to avoid misunderstandings and promote a positive work environment.

3. Motivation and Rewards

Motivational factors can vary significantly between regions. In Western countries, employees are often motivated by individual achievement, career progression, and financial rewards. In contrast, in many Asian cultures, motivation may stem from collective success, job stability, and a sense of belonging to a group or organization.

Regional HR practices should reflect these differences in motivation. Incentive programs in one country might focus on individual performance, while in another, collective achievements or team-based rewards may be more effective.

4. Work-Life Balance

Expectations around work-life balance differ globally. In countries like France, strict labour laws mandate shorter working hours and extensive vacation time. However, in countries such as South Korea or Japan, longer working hours are culturally ingrained, and employees often feel an obligation to stay at the office beyond official hours.

HR policies must account for these regional differences. While encouraging work-life balance is a global priority, the approach to achieving it may vary. In regions where long hours are the norm, HR might focus on wellness programs or flexible hours, whereas in countries with regulated working hours, they could emphasize productivity during shorter workdays.

Training and Development in Regional Contexts

Training and development programs are essential for workforce growth, but their design and delivery must consider regional nuances. In Western countries, employees often value personalized learning paths, such as online modules or workshops focused on individual skill-building. In contrast, in regions like Asia or Africa, collective learning experiences such as team-based training sessions or mentoring programs are more culturally aligned. Furthermore, the content of training programs may differ—Western organizations might prioritize leadership development and innovation, while companies in developing markets may focus on foundational skills and technical training to address local workforce needs. By tailoring training programs to fit regional learning styles and priorities, organizations can build a more competent and engaged global workforce.

Adapting Global Strategies to Regional Realities

One of the major challenges of managing a global workforce is creating a cohesive HR strategy that respects local differences while ensuring a unified corporate culture. Here are strategies HR professionals can use to adapt global practices to regional needs:

1. Cultural Awareness Training:

Before implementing any policy, HR professionals need to be culturally aware. Providing cultural training to global teams ensures that employees and managers understand the values and expectations of their colleagues in different regions. This training can help avoid conflicts, foster better collaboration, and improve overall communication.

2. Tailoring Policies to Fit Local Contexts:

Global policies should serve as broad guidelines, but local teams should have the flexibility to adapt these policies to their unique cultural and legal environments. For example, while a global performance review system might set out common metrics, the way reviews are conducted may need to vary. In some cultures, face-to-face feedback may be valued, while in others, written reviews might be preferred.

3. Regional HR Leaders:

Appointing regional HR leaders who understand both the global goals of the organization and the local culture can bridge the gap between global strategy and local execution. These leaders can help ensure that policies are implemented in a culturally sensitive way while maintaining alignment with the company's overall objectives.

4. Global-Local Balance:

Achieving a balance between global standardization and local customization is key. Certain core HR practices—such as compliance with international labour laws, ethical standards, and diversity goals—should be upheld across all regions. However, flexibility in areas like employee engagement, reward systems, and leadership styles allows the company to respect and integrate regional nuances.

Case Study: A Global Company's Approach to Regional HR

Let's consider the example of a multinational corporation operating in North America, Europe, and Southeast Asia. This company faces challenges such as varying labour laws, cultural differences in communication, and different expectations for employee engagement.

In the U.S., the company's HR team focuses on promoting individual performance and providing financial incentives for employees who exceed their targets. However, in their Southeast Asian offices, the HR team emphasizes teamwork and collective achievement, with group-based rewards and recognition programs.

The company also tailors its leadership development programs to fit regional needs. In Europe, leaders are trained in collaborative management techniques, while in their Asian branches, managers are coached on maintaining hierarchy while fostering innovation.

By adapting their global HR practices to regional needs, this company successfully creates a unified corporate culture that respects local values and engages employees across different markets.

Regional HR Practices in Asia: Balancing Collectivism and Global Standards

Asia is a region known for its collectivist culture, where teamwork and group harmony are prioritized over individual achievement. In countries like Japan, South Korea, and China, organizations often face the challenge of aligning global HR strategies that emphasize individual performance with local values that favor collective success.

Example: Adapting Performance Management in Japan

In Japan, global companies that implement performance-based systems often face resistance because the culture places high value on group harmony and consensus-building. To overcome this challenge, HR professionals in Japan adapt global performance management systems by incorporating team-based evaluations. Rather than solely focusing on individual KPIs, HR teams evaluate employees based on their contributions to group success. This approach respects Japan's collectivist culture while ensuring that global performance standards are still met.

Another adaptation is in feedback delivery. In Japan, direct criticism is often seen as disruptive to harmony, so HR professionals ensure that performance feedback is delivered more indirectly and respectfully, allowing employees to maintain face while still addressing areas for improvement.

HR Practices in Europe: Balancing Employee Rights with Global Flexibility

Europe's labour laws and strong worker protections pose unique challenges for multinational companies.

In countries like France, Germany, and Sweden, labour unions play a significant role in shaping HR policies, and organizations must navigate strict regulations that protect employees' rights. This requires HR teams to balance global strategies for flexibility and innovation with local compliance requirements.

Example: Navigating Labour Laws in France

In France, the labour code is known for being particularly stringent, with rules governing everything from working hours to employee dismissals. Global companies must adapt their HR practices to ensure compliance with these laws while still fostering a dynamic work environment. For example, while flexible working hours are a key component of global HR strategies, in France, HR must ensure that these policies comply with strict regulations regarding overtime and working hours.

HR professionals in France also work closely with labour unions to implement global talent management strategies. For instance, global companies may want to introduce performance-based promotions, but in France, these policies must be negotiated with union representatives to ensure they align with national labour standards. This collaborative approach helps HR teams maintain global standards while respecting local labour dynamics.

HR Practices in the Middle East: Navigating Cultural Norms and Gender Inclusion

The Middle East presents unique HR challenges due to its conservative cultural norms and varying degrees of gender inclusion. In countries like Saudi Arabia and the UAE, HR professionals must carefully adapt global diversity and inclusion strategies to fit local cultural expectations.

Example: Gender Inclusion in Saudi Arabia

Saudi Arabia's Vision 2030 has led to significant changes in the country's labour market, particularly in terms of women's participation. Global companies operating in Saudi Arabia have adapted their HR strategies to align with the country's evolving policies on gender inclusion. For instance, multinational companies may have global diversity goals that require equal representation of men and women in leadership roles. In Saudi Arabia, HR teams are adapting these goals by creating women's leadership programs that comply with local norms, such as providing separate facilities for male and female employees where required.

Additionally, HR professionals in Saudi Arabia ensure that global gender diversity programs respect Islamic cultural practices, such as maintaining dress codes and segregation in certain settings. By adapting these strategies, companies can support gender inclusion without conflicting with local cultural norms.

HR Practices in Africa: Bridging Skill Gaps While Adhering to Global Standards

Africa is a continent with vast potential, but also significant challenges in terms of education and workforce development. In countries like South Africa and Nigeria, HR professionals must adapt global talent development strategies to address local skill gaps and workforce readiness.

Example: Skills Development in South Africa

A shortage of skilled workers in key industries characterizes South Africa's labour market. Global companies that operate in South Africa often face the challenge of implementing global HR strategies that rely on highly skilled employees. To bridge this gap, HR professionals adapt global talent development programs by investing heavily in local skills development initiatives.

For instance, companies may partner with local universities to offer internships, apprenticeships, and training programs that equip young professionals with the skills needed to meet global standards. These initiatives not only help multinational companies meet their workforce needs but also contribute to the development of local talent, aligning with South Africa's national goals for workforce development.

Adapting global HR strategies to local realities is crucial for multinational companies aiming for success in diverse regions. In today's interconnected world, businesses must operate seamlessly across borders while respecting the unique cultural, legal, and social landscapes of each country. For instance, aligning performance management practices in Japan requires sensitivity to hierarchical structures and a collectivist mindset, while navigating labour laws in France demands a deep understanding of worker protections and union dynamics. Similarly, promoting gender inclusion in Saudi Arabia involves working within the framework of cultural and societal norms, and bridging skill gaps in South Africa necessitates targeted strategies for education and workforce development. HR professionals are at the forefront of these challenges, acting as strategic enablers to ensure global standards are upheld while local nuances are respected. By mastering this balancing act, organizations can achieve a competitive advantage and foster meaningful employee engagement.

Understanding and adapting to regional HR practices is not just an operational necessity but a strategic imperative for any globally operating organization. Differences in cultural values, legal frameworks, and societal expectations significantly influence how employees communicate, collaborate, and work towards shared goals. For example, while some cultures may prioritize individual achievement, others may value teamwork and collective success. HR professionals must develop adaptive strategies that integrate global objectives with local realities, ensuring that employees feel both valued and understood. Flexible policies, inclusive practices, and an openness to regional diversity can help create a harmonious and productive global workforce. Beyond operational efficiency, embracing cultural diversity becomes a source of innovation, creativity, and competitive strength, empowering organizations to thrive in an increasingly complex global market. By addressing these challenges head-on, businesses can turn regional diversity into a powerful driver of innovation and sustainable growth.

PART II:

Technological Evolution and Workforce Innovation

"Navigating the crossroads of culture and HR is the key to transforming organizational challenges into enduring success."

CHAPTER 12

Cultural Influences on HR:

Navigating the intersection of culture and Organizational Success

In today's globalized business environment, understanding cultural differences is paramount for organizations operating across borders. Human Resources (HR) practices must be adapted to meet the needs of diverse workforces shaped by their cultural backgrounds. Culture influences everything from communication styles and leadership preferences to performance management and employee motivation.

Human Resources (HR) practices are profoundly shaped by the cultural contexts in which they operate. As organizations expand globally, HR professionals face the challenge of adapting policies and practices to align with the cultural norms, values, and expectations of different regions. Culture plays a pivotal role in shaping employee behaviours, leadership styles, communication preferences, and organizational structures, making it essential for HR to understand and manage these influences effectively.

This chapter examines the various cultural factors that impact HR practices, offering insights into how organizations can navigate these complexities. It also delves into various cultural dimensions and how they impact HR strategies, drawing on frameworks such as Hofstede's Cultural Dimensions and other key cultural concepts.

1. The Influence of National Culture on HR Practices

One of the most significant cultural influences on HR is the national culture in which an organization operates. National culture affects everything from work ethics and communication styles to leadership preferences and employee motivation. Geert Hofstede's Cultural Dimensions framework offers a useful lens through which to understand these differences, with dimensions such as power distance, individualism versus collectivism, and uncertainty avoidance shaping workplace behaviours.

Power Distance and Hierarchical Structures

In countries with high power distance, such as India, Mexico, and Russia, hierarchical structures are deeply ingrained, and employees are more likely to defer to authority figures. In these cultures, HR practices must accommodate the expectation that decisions are made at the top, and employees may be less likely to challenge their superiors or offer feedback. HR policies that involve participatory decision-making or flat organizational structures may not resonate as effectively in these environments.

Conversely, in low power-distance countries such as Denmark or New Zealand, HR professionals must adopt more egalitarian approaches. Employees in these cultures expect open communication and a greater degree of autonomy, making it essential for HR teams to foster an inclusive and participatory work environment.

Individualism vs. Collectivism

Another critical dimension is the individualism-collectivism scale. In highly individualistic cultures, such as the United States or Australia, HR practices emphasize personal achievement, merit-based rewards, and individual performance evaluations. Employees are motivated by personal success and are more likely to prioritize their own career development over collective goals.

In contrast, in collectivist cultures like China, South Korea, and many African countries, HR must focus on team dynamics, group harmony, and collective achievements. Performance evaluations may be team-based rather than individual, and rewards are often distributed equally to promote group cohesion. HR professionals in these environments must carefully align incentives with the cultural emphasis on collective success rather than individual recognition.

2. The Role of Religion in Shaping HR Policies

Religion is a powerful cultural influence that plays a significant role in shaping HR practices, particularly in regions where religious beliefs are deeply integrated into daily life. Religion not only affects the way employees approach work but also influences how organizations structure their policies, offer support, and create inclusive environments. In countries such as Saudi Arabia, India, and Indonesia, religion can significantly impact work schedules, dress codes, holidays, workplace interactions, and even conflict resolution. As a result, HR professionals must consider religious beliefs and practices when developing policies to ensure that they are both culturally sensitive and aligned with local norms.

Example: Religious Practices in the Middle East

In many countries in the Middle East, including Saudi Arabia, the UAE, and Qatar, Islam plays a central role in the lives of both employees and employers. This profound religious influence often requires HR departments to implement specific practices to accommodate employees' religious needs and observances. For example, daily prayer times are an essential part of the Islamic faith, and employees may need to take time off during the day to pray. In response, many companies provide dedicated prayer spaces, allowing Muslim employees to fulfil their religious duties without affecting their work performance. HR teams also adjust work schedules during Ramadan, the Islamic holy month of fasting, to accommodate shorter working hours and provide meal breaks after sunset.

Moreover, in countries like Saudi Arabia, gender-specific policies may be necessary due to cultural norms and religious practices. For instance, workplaces may need to establish gender-segregated areas, including separate offices, prayer rooms, or restrooms, in line with Islamic customs. HR professionals must navigate these religious and cultural norms while also aligning with global diversity and inclusion initiatives. This may require careful consideration to ensure that employees feel respected while maintaining a balance with international standards of equality.

Example: Religious Practices in India

India is a diverse country with multiple religious beliefs and practices coexisting, including Hinduism, Islam, Christianity, Sikhism, and others. This religious diversity significantly impacts HR policies, particularly in relation to holidays, dietary restrictions, and dress codes. For instance, during religious festivals like Diwali, Eid, and Christmas, employees often expect time off to observe these significant occasions with their families. HR teams must ensure that holiday policies reflect these needs while balancing the operational requirements of the business. Similarly, many employees in India may observe dietary restrictions based on their religion, such as vegetarianism in Hinduism or halal dietary laws in Islam. HR professionals need to be sensitive to these practices and ensure that workplace meals and events are inclusive and respectful of all religious dietary restrictions.

Religious dress codes also play a role in shaping HR practices in India. For instance, many Hindu women may prefer to wear sarees or salwar kameez, while Muslim women may wear hijabs or other modest clothing, and Sikh men may wear turbans. HR teams must ensure that workplace attire policies are respectful of these religious dress codes while maintaining professionalism in the workplace.

Example: Religious Practices in Southeast Asia

In countries like Indonesia, where Islam is the dominant religion, HR policies must also reflect the religious needs of employees. During Ramadan, for instance, HR departments often adjust work hours to allow for fasting schedules and offer flexibility in break times for prayer and meal preparation after sunset. Similarly, companies in Indonesia may provide employees with prayer rooms and encourage religious observance during the workday, ensuring that employees feel supported in their spiritual practices. In addition, Islamic holidays such as Eid al-Fitr and Eid al-Adha are significant events, and HR departments typically provide time off for these celebrations, allowing employees to spend time with their families and communities.

Balancing Global HR Standards with Religious Sensitivity

While religion plays an essential role in shaping HR practices in many regions, HR professionals must also ensure that these religious accommodations align with the company's broader global HR strategy. This balance can be challenging, especially for multinational companies with diverse workforces. For example, while accommodating religious observances is crucial in certain regions, organizations must also ensure that these accommodations do not inadvertently create division or inequality within the workplace. The key is to promote an environment of respect and inclusion, where religious practices are honored without compromising organizational goals or creating a divide between employees of different faiths.

In some cases, multinational companies implement flexible holiday policies that allow employees to choose which holidays they observe, regardless of their religious background. This approach can foster inclusivity by respecting all religious and cultural celebrations while maintaining the flexibility needed to meet the company's operational needs. Similarly, HR policies may include education and training programs aimed at fostering greater religious awareness and understanding among employees, encouraging respect for diversity and promoting harmonious working relationships.

Religion is a powerful force that shapes HR policies in many parts of the world, influencing everything from employee schedules and holiday observances to workplace attire and dietary practices. By taking into account the religious needs and practices of employees, HR professionals can create policies that reflect both local cultural values and global corporate objectives. By doing so, companies can foster an inclusive and respectful environment that enables employees to feel supported in their religious beliefs while contributing to the organization's success . The challenge for HR teams is to balance religious sensitivity with the company's overarching goals, ensuring that policies are inclusive without sacrificing operational efficiency or unity across a diverse workforce.

3. Communication Styles and HR's Role in Bridging Gaps

Communication styles vary widely across cultures, and HR professionals must be adept at managing these differences to prevent misunderstandings and ensure effective collaboration. In high-context cultures, such as those in Japan or Brazil, much of the communication is implicit, and employees rely on non-verbal cues, context, and relationships to convey meaning. In these environments, HR professionals need to ensure that communication strategies are nuanced and culturally appropriate, avoiding direct confrontation and fostering harmony.

In low-context cultures, such as the United States or Germany, communication is typically more direct, with a greater emphasis on clarity and explicit messaging. HR teams in these regions must prioritize transparency, clear guidelines, and direct feedback to meet employee expectations.

Case Study: Cross-Cultural Communication in Multinational Teams

A global tech company with teams in Germany, Japan, and the United States faced challenges with cross-cultural communication. While the German team preferred direct and concise communication, the Japanese team valued indirect and relationship-based interactions. To address this, HR implemented cross-cultural training programs that helped employees understand each other's communication styles and adjust their approaches accordingly. The result was improved collaboration and fewer misunderstandings, fostering a more cohesive and productive work environment.

4. Labour Laws and Local Regulations

Cultural norms heavily influence local labour laws and regulations, and HR teams must navigate these frameworks to ensure compliance while aligning with global standards. In regions like Europe, where worker protections are strong, HR professionals must develop strategies that respect employee rights while promoting organizational flexibility.

Example: Labour Laws in Europe

In countries like France and Germany, HR teams face strict regulations regarding working hours, employee benefits, and termination policies. For instance, in France, the 35-hour workweek and robust employee protections make it challenging for companies to implement global flexibility strategies like remote work or overtime policies. HR professionals must work closely with labour unions and ensure that any global strategies are tailored to comply with local laws.

In contrast, in countries like the United States, where labour laws are more flexible, HR can more easily implement global strategies that promote agile work environments, such as at-will employment and flexible work schedules.

5. Generational Differences and HR Strategy

Generational diversity within a culture can also impact HR practices, as different age groups bring varying expectations and values to the workplace. In many countries, younger generations tend to prioritize work-life balance, purpose-driven careers, and flexible working conditions, while older generations may value job security, stability, and traditional hierarchical structures.

Example: Generational Shifts in India

In India, younger employees are increasingly seeking flexibility, remote work options, and opportunities for personal growth. They prioritize companies that align with their values and offer opportunities for innovation. On the other hand, older employees may place a greater emphasis on job security, loyalty, and respect for authority. HR professionals in India must balance these generational expectations by creating policies that appeal to both younger and older employees, ensuring that organizational culture evolves without alienating any group.

Hofstede's Cultural Dimensions Applied to HR

Geert Hofstede's model offers a valuable lens through which to understand cultural differences in the workplace. Hofstede identified six dimensions that impact how employees view authority, individual achievement, and organizational practices. These dimensions are:

1. Power Distance – The extent to which less powerful members of an organization expect and accept unequal power distribution.

2. Individualism vs. Collectivism – The degree to which individuals are integrated into groups or expected to stand alone.

3. Masculinity vs. Femininity – The preference for achievement, heroism, and material rewards versus cooperation, modesty, and quality of life.

4. Uncertainty Avoidance – The level of discomfort a society feels about uncertainty and ambiguity.

5. Long-term vs. Short-term Orientation – The focus on future rewards and persistence versus immediate results and quick outcomes.

6. Indulgence vs. Restraint – The extent to which societies allow for relatively free gratification of basic human desires.

By applying these dimensions, HR departments can craft policies that align with local norms and practices. For instance, in high power distance countries like India, employees may expect clear hierarchies and respect for authority. In contrast in low power-distance countries such as Sweden, flatter organizational structures and participative management may be preferred.

High-context vs. Low-context Cultures

Communication plays a crucial role in the effectiveness of HR strategies, and its impact varies significantly between high-context and low-context cultures.

High-context cultures, such as Japan and many Middle Eastern countries, rely heavily on non-verbal cues, shared experiences, and implicit understanding in communication. Relationships are paramount, and much of what is conveyed remains unspoken. HR professionals in these cultures must prioritize relationship-building, trust, and subtlety in communication.

Low-context cultures, like the U.S. and Germany, depend on explicit, clear communication where the message is conveyed directly in words. Transparency, written contracts, and clear expectations are the norm. HR managers in these settings need to ensure that policies, performance expectations, and feedback mechanisms are articulated clearly to avoid misunderstandings.

Individualism vs. Collectivism

Aspect	Individualistic Culture (e.g., U.S., Canada)	Collectivist Culture (e.g., China, Japan),
Values	Personal achievement, independence, self-reliance,	Group harmony, loyalty, teamwork
HR Policies	Personal development plans, performance-based incentives, merit-based promotions	Emphasis on group achievements, employee well-being, long-term stability
Employee Approach	Encouraged to take ownership of their careers, rewarded for individual success	Teams are cohesive, decisions made with conseus, rewards favor collective outcomes

The contrast between individualistic and collectivist cultures is another key factor in shaping HR practices.

Individualistic cultures (e.g., U.S., Canada) emphasize personal achievement, independence, and self-reliance. HR policies here may focus on personal development plans, performance-based incentives, and merit-based promotions. Employees are encouraged to take ownership of their careers and are rewarded for individual success.

Collectivist cultures (e.g., China, Japan) prioritize group harmony, loyalty, and teamwork. In such environments, HR practices will emphasize group achievements, employee well-being, and long-term stability. Teams are more cohesive, and decisions are often made with consensus. Reward systems in collectivist cultures may favor collective outcomes over individual contributions.

Power Distance

Power distance reflects the extent to which people accept hierarchical structures in organizations and society. This concept has direct implications for leadership styles and HR management.

In high power distance cultures, such as in many Asian and Latin American countries, authority figures are respected, and decisions are often made top-down. HR practices in these cultures should maintain clear lines of authority, with senior management playing a prominent role in decision-making. Formality is usually expected, and employees may be less likely to question directives from superiors.

In low power distance cultures, like those in Northern Europe, hierarchy is less pronounced, and collaboration across levels of the organization is encouraged. HR professionals may implement flatter organizational structures, foster open communication, and encourage employees to contribute ideas regardless of their rank.

Understanding power distance helps HR professionals decide the appropriate leadership development programs, employee engagement strategies, and conflict resolution approaches that will resonate with their workforce.

Uncertainty Avoidance

Uncertainty avoidance addresses how comfortable a culture is with ambiguity, change, and risk.

High uncertainty avoidance cultures (e.g., Greece, Japan) value stability, predictability, and clear rules. HR policies in these settings should focus on creating structured environments with well-defined roles, responsibilities, and procedures. Employees may prefer job security and be resistant to change, requiring HR to carefully manage transitions and organizational changes.

Low uncertainty avoidance cultures (e.g., Singapore, the UK) are more tolerant of ambiguity and innovation. HR can encourage a more flexible, dynamic approach to work, with fewer rigid guidelines. Employees in these cultures may be more open to change and experimentation, allowing organizations to foster creativity and adaptability.

Long-term vs. Short-term Orientation

Aspect	Long-term Oriented Culture (e.g., China, South Korea)	Short-term Oriented Culture (e.g., U.S., Nigeria),
Values	Perseverance, thrift, sustained effort towards future goals	Quick results, immediate outcomes
HR Focus	Long-term career development, employee loyalty, continuous improvement	Short-term performance metrics, bonuses, immediate rewards
HR Practices	Succession planning, employee retention	Faster career progression, rapid recognition

Cultural attitudes toward time—whether a society prioritizes long-term planning or short-term results—also influence HR strategies.

Long-term oriented cultures (e.g., China, South Korea) value perseverance, thrift, and sustained effort toward future goals. In these cultures, HR may emphasize long-term career development, employee loyalty, and investments in continuous improvement. Succession planning and employee retention are critical.

Short-term oriented cultures (e.g., the U.S., Nigeria) prioritize quick results and immediate outcomes. HR strategies may focus on short-term performance metrics, bonuses, and more immediate rewards for success. Employees in these environments may expect faster career progression and rapid recognition for their achievements.

Balancing long-term objectives with short-term gains can help HR managers create a sustainable work environment while meeting immediate organizational goals.

Cultural influences on HR practices shape everything from communication styles and leadership preferences to employee motivation and regulatory compliance. By understanding these influences, HR professionals can develop strategies that respect local cultures while aligning with global goals. Adapting HR practices to cultural realities is essential for fostering a productive, inclusive work environment. Frameworks like Hofstede's cultural dimensions and concepts like high- and low-context communication help HR professionals design policies that align with employees' cultural values and expectations. This cultural sensitivity improves employee engagement and satisfaction while enhancing organizational effectiveness.

"Leveraging technology in global HR drives workforce transformation, empowering organizations to thrive in a dynamic digital era."

CHAPTER 13

Technology and the Evolution of Global HR :

Empowering Workforce Transformation in a Digital World

In an era where digital transformation is reshaping industries globally, the role of technology in Human Resources (HR) management has evolved into a critical enabler of organizational success. Technology is not just a tool but a powerful driver of workforce transformation, enabling HR to navigate the complexities of a globalized business environment. The convergence of HR Information Systems (HRIS), Artificial Intelligence (AI), and Machine Learning (ML) has allowed HR to become more data-driven, efficient, and strategic. However, as HR technologies transcend borders, issues of data privacy and security have emerged as paramount concerns. These technologies are revolutionizing HR globally, while also addressing the complexities of managing data across different regulatory landscapes.

The rapid evolution of technology has revolutionized the way HR operates on a global scale. From AI-powered recruitment processes to cloud-based HR management systems, technology is enabling organizations to transform their workforce strategies and drive efficiency, innovation, and growth.

In this chapter, we examine how HR professionals are utilizing technology to navigate the complexities of managing a global workforce and empowering employees in a digital environment.

HR Information Systems (HRIS) on a Global Scale

HR Information Systems (HRIS) have become the backbone of modern HR functions, integrating various HR processes—from recruitment to payroll—into a single platform. On a global scale, HRIS plays a crucial role in managing diverse workforces spread across multiple geographies, each with its unique labour laws, compliance requirements, and cultural nuances.

Global HRIS allows organizations to maintain consistency in HR practices while accommodating local variations. For instance, while a multinational company can standardize talent management processes, it can also customize payroll and benefits administration based on local labour regulations. These systems enable real-time reporting and analytics, helping HR leaders make data-driven decisions that align with global and regional objectives.

However, implementing a global HRIS presents challenges, such as ensuring system compatibility across different countries, managing multicurrency payrolls, and navigating legal restrictions on data transfer. Additionally, cultural differences in employee expectations and performance management approaches must be taken into account when designing HRIS modules. A well-implemented HRIS ensures not only operational efficiency but also the ability to support a globally dispersed workforce effectively.

HR Information Systems (HRIS) have become indispensable tools for global organizations, providing a centralized platform for managing employee data, payroll, benefits, and performance evaluations across different regions. HRIS provide the flexibility and scalability necessary to accommodate regional variations in labour laws, tax regulations, and cultural differences, while maintaining a unified global HR strategy.

Example: Cloud-Based HRIS in Multinational Corporations

A global manufacturing company, with offices in over 30 countries, faced significant challenges in managing employee data and compliance with local labour laws. By implementing a cloud-based HRIS system, the company streamlined its HR processes and ensured consistency across its global workforce. The system allowed HR professionals in different regions to access real-time data, manage payroll according to local tax regulations, and ensure compliance with labour laws, all while maintaining a centralized global HR strategy.

Cloud-based HRIS systems also enabled the company to provide a consistent employee experience across all regions. Employees could access their benefits, performance reviews, and training materials through a single platform, regardless of their location. This digital transformation not only improved operational efficiency but also enhanced employee engagement and satisfaction.

AI and Machine Learning in HR Processes

The integration of AI and machine learning (ML) into HR processes marks a significant leap toward intelligent workforce management. AI-driven solutions are reshaping key HR functions such as recruitment, performance management, employee engagement, and talent development.

1. AI in Recruitment: AI-powered algorithms are being used to automate the hiring process, from candidate screening to interview scheduling. By analyzing candidate profiles, AI can identify the best talent matches, reducing time-to-hire and enhancing the quality of hires. Machine learning models can continuously improve by learning from past recruitment successes and failures, refining criteria to predict the most suitable candidates for a role.

2. Performance Management: AI tools can analyze large datasets on employee performance and provide insights into individual strengths, weaknesses, and potential career trajectories. Predictive analytics enables HR to forecast future performance trends and

identify high-potential employees. Machine learning models can suggest personalized training programs or development opportunities based on an employee's past performance and learning patterns.

3. Employee Engagement and Retention: AI-powered platforms can monitor employee sentiment in real-time through surveys, social interactions, and work patterns. By identifying patterns of disengagement, HR can proactively address issues before they escalate, fostering a healthier work environment and improving retention rates.

4. Learning and Development: AI facilitates the creation of personalized learning pathways for employees, providing recommendations tailored to their role, performance data, and future career aspirations. This not only enhances employee satisfaction but also drives organizational growth by upskilling the workforce in line with evolving business needs.

However, while AI and ML offer enormous potential for enhancing HR functions, there are ethical considerations. These include biases in AI algorithms that may perpetuate inequality in hiring or performance evaluations. HR professionals must ensure that AI tools are used ethically, with constant oversight to prevent discriminatory practices.

Artificial intelligence (AI) and machine learning are revolutionizing HR processes by automating repetitive tasks, streamlining recruitment, and delivering data-driven insights. AI-powered tools are being used to screen resumes, assess candidate skills, and predict employee performance, allowing HR professionals to focus on strategic decision-making and talent development.

Example: AI in Recruitment at a Global Tech Firm

A global tech company, facing high volumes of job applications across multiple regions, implemented an AI-driven recruitment platform to streamline its hiring process. The platform used natural language processing (NLP) to scan and analyze resumes, identifying the most qualified candidates based on specific job criteria. This significantly reduced the time spent on manual resume reviews, allowing the HR team to focus on interviewing top candidates.

In addition, the AI platform assessed candidates' soft skills by analyzing their communication style and problem-solving abilities during interviews. This data-driven approach helped the company identify candidates who not only had the technical skills required for the role but also fit the company's culture and values. By leveraging AI, the company improved the efficiency of its recruitment process while making more informed hiring decisions.

Data Privacy and Security Across Borders

As global HR becomes increasingly reliant on technology, the issue of data privacy and security has taken center stage. With personal employee data being stored, processed, and transferred across borders, organizations face significant challenges in maintaining compliance with various international data protection laws.

The General Data Protection Regulation (GDPR) in Europe is one of the most stringent data privacy laws, and it applies to any company that processes the data of EU citizens, regardless of the company's location. Similarly, countries such as Brazil, Canada, and Japan have enacted their own data privacy regulations, often with unique compliance requirements. For multinational companies, ensuring that their HR practices align with these diverse legal frameworks is crucial.

Data breaches in HR systems can have severe consequences, ranging from legal penalties to damage to an organization's reputation. Therefore, HR leaders must work closely with IT and legal teams to establish robust data security protocols, including encryption, access controls, and data anonymization techniques. It's also important to regularly audit data practices to ensure compliance with local and international regulations.

Moreover, employee consent must be obtained for the collection and use of personal data, and employees should be informed about how their data is being stored and used. Transparency in data handling is key to building trust with employees, particularly in a world where data breaches and cyberattacks are increasingly common.

Technology is transforming the HR landscape, enabling organizations to manage a global workforce with unprecedented efficiency and precision. HR Information

Systems streamline processes across borders, while AI and machine learning enhance decision-making and drive workforce transformation. However, as technology continues to shape HR, data privacy and security challenges must be addressed to protect employee information and comply with global regulations.

As HR teams increasingly rely on digital platforms to manage employee data, data privacy and security have become critical concerns, particularly for global organizations that operate across multiple jurisdictions with varying data protection laws. The European Union's General Data Protection Regulation (GDPR) and other data privacy regulations require HR professionals to implement robust security measures to protect employee data and ensure compliance with local laws.

Example: GDPR Compliance in a Global Organization

A global retail company, operating in both the European Union and the United States, faced challenges in ensuring compliance with GDPR while managing employee data across different regions. The company's HR team worked closely with its legal and IT departments to implement a data management system that complied with GDPR requirements, including obtaining employee consent for data processing and ensuring data encryption.

The company also implemented data localization measures, storing European employee data on servers located within the European Union (EU) to comply with the GDPR's data transfer regulations. By prioritizing data privacy and security, the company not only avoided costly penalties but also built trust with its employees, who felt confident that their personal information was being handled securely.

The Impact of Technology on Employee Engagement and Learning

Technology has also transformed the way organizations engage with employees and deliver training and development programs. Learning management systems (LMS) and virtual training platforms enable companies to deliver consistent learning experiences to employees across various regions, regardless of their physical location. Gamification, microlearning, and AI-driven learning paths are becoming popular tools for delivering personalized and engaging learning experiences.

Example: Virtual Learning and Development at a Global Financial Institution

A global financial institution implemented a virtual learning platform to provide consistent training and development opportunities to its employees across 40 countries. The platform used AI to create personalized learning paths based on each employee's role, skills, and career goals. Employees could access training modules, webinars, and interactive learning sessions from any device, allowing them to develop new skills and advance their careers.

The platform also incorporated gamification elements, such as leaderboards and rewards, to encourage employee participation and engagement. As a result, the company saw a significant increase in employee satisfaction and retention, as employees felt empowered to take control of their learning and career development.

The Role of HR in Managing the Digital Workforce

As organizations adopt digital tools and platforms to manage their workforce, HR professionals play a critical role in ensuring that these technologies are implemented effectively and that employees are empowered to succeed in a digital work environment. This includes providing training on new technologies, fostering a culture of digital literacy, and ensuring that digital tools align with the organization's overall HR strategy.

Example: Digital Literacy Initiatives at a Global Consumer Goods Company

A global consumer goods company, with a large workforce spread across multiple regions, recognized the need to improve digital literacy among its employees to ensure the success of its digital transformation initiatives. The company's HR team implemented a series of digital literacy workshops and training programs to help employees develop the skills needed to use new technologies effectively.

In addition to technical training, the HR team focused on fostering a culture of continuous learning and innovation, encouraging employees to adopt new technologies and explore ways to enhance their work processes. By investing in digital literacy, the company ensured that its workforce was equipped to thrive in a digital work environment and contribute to the company's overall success.

Technology is playing a transformative role in HR, enabling organizations to manage their global workforce more efficiently, enhance employee engagement, and drive innovation. From AI-powered recruitment to cloud-based HRIS, the digital tools available to HR professionals are helping organizations navigate the complexities of managing a global workforce. By embracing these technologies and addressing challenges such as data privacy and digital literacy, HR professionals can empower their workforce and drive organizational success in a digital world.

HR leaders must embrace these technologies while remaining vigilant about their ethical implications and legal responsibilities. By doing so, they can leverage technology to empower a truly global workforce, creating a workplace that is not only more efficient but also more secure and inclusive in the digital age.

"Remote work is reshaping boundaries, fostering a borderless workforce that redefines collaboration in a globalized world."

CHAPTER 14

Remote Work and the Borderless Workforce :

Redefining collaboration in a Globalized Era

The rise of remote work has revolutionized the modern workplace, erasing geographical barriers and redefining the concept of a "borderless workforce." This new concept of a borderless workforce has redefined how organizations operate in today's globalized era. Technology has enabled employees to work from virtually anywhere, allowing companies to access talent across geographical boundaries. As organizations increasingly adopt flexible work models, they are tapping into global talent pools while adapting to new challenges in managing virtual teams, ensuring engagement, and maintaining productivity across different time zones.

This shift presents both opportunities and challenges for HR professionals, who must navigate issues such as managing virtual teams, global talent acquisition, and maintaining employee engagement across time zones.

This chapter examines how HR leaders can navigate these shifts, from building high-performing virtual teams to successfully recruiting and engaging talent on a global scale. It also examines how organizations are adapting to this new reality and offers examples of effective strategies for managing a remote and borderless workforce.

Managing Virtual Teams Across Borders

One of the key challenges in managing a remote workforce is fostering collaboration and productivity among virtual teams that are spread across different regions and time zones. While remote work offers flexibility, it also requires HR professionals to implement strategies that ensure seamless communication and teamwork, regardless of physical location.

Example: Asynchronous Communication at a Global Software Company

A global software company with employees in the United States, India, and Europe faced challenges coordinating meetings and project timelines due to the time zone differences. To address this, the HR team implemented an asynchronous communication model, where team members could contribute to projects at their own pace, regardless of their time zone. By using tools like Slack, Trello, and shared Google Docs, employees were able to collaborate effectively without needing to be online simultaneously.

This approach allowed the team to maximize productivity, with work progressing around the clock as team members in different time zones completed their tasks. The HR team also provided training on best practices for asynchronous communication, ensuring that employees were comfortable using the tools and understood how to keep projects on track.

Managing Virtual Teams

Managing virtual teams requires a shift in leadership strategies and HR practices. Unlike traditional teams that operate in the same physical space, virtual teams are dispersed across various locations, often with little or no in-person interaction. For HR professionals and team leaders, this presents unique challenges in fostering collaboration, maintaining communication, and building trust.

1. Communication and Collaboration Tools:

One of the most critical components of managing virtual teams is ensuring seamless communication. With team members often working asynchronously, leveraging the right digital tools is essential. Platforms like Slack, Microsoft Teams, and Zoom have become indispensable for real-time communication and collaboration. Additionally, project management tools such as Trello, Asana, and Monday.com help teams stay aligned on tasks and goals, regardless of time zones.

2. Building Trust and Team Cohesion:

Trust is the foundation of any successful team, but building it in virtual environments requires intentional effort. Virtual leaders must be proactive in fostering a sense of belonging, encouraging open communication, and recognizing the contributions of each team member. Regular check-ins, team-building activities, and creating opportunities for informal interactions, such as virtual coffee breaks, can strengthen relationships and reduce feelings of isolation.

3. Leadership and Accountability:

Managing a remote workforce requires a leadership style that emphasizes empowerment and results over micromanagement. Leaders must set clear expectations, provide regular feedback, and hold team members accountable for their work. A results-oriented approach, where success is measured by outcomes rather than time spent working, fosters autonomy and trust in virtual teams. Leaders must also be sensitive to cultural differences, communication styles, and varying work preferences across diverse teams.

Global Talent Acquisition in a Remote World

The rise of remote work has opened up new opportunities for organizations to tap into a global talent pool. HR professionals no longer need to limit their search for talent to specific geographic locations; instead, they can hire the best candidates regardless of their location. However, this also means that HR must navigate different labour laws, compensation structures, and cultural differences when hiring employees from different regions.

1. Recruiting Beyond Borders:

The remote work revolution enables organizations to assemble truly diverse teams by recruiting talent from different countries, cultures, and backgrounds. However, global talent acquisition also comes with its own set of challenges. HR teams must navigate varying labour laws, tax regulations, and compliance requirements across different countries. Moreover, the recruitment process itself may need to be adjusted for global talent pools, with virtual interviews becoming the norm and time zone differences considered when scheduling meetings.

2. Cultural Competency and Inclusion:

Hiring a globally distributed team necessitates a deep understanding of cultural differences. HR professionals must cultivate cultural competency to create an inclusive recruitment process and ensure that all candidates feel valued, regardless of their background. Inclusivity should extend beyond recruitment and into onboarding, where cultural awareness training and support for international employees can help foster a positive employee experience.

3. Onboarding Remote Talent:

Onboarding is a critical phase in integrating new hires into the organization. With remote teams, traditional onboarding processes must be adapted to virtual environments. Creating a structured and engaging remote onboarding experience is essential, with clear guidelines, access to digital resources, and opportunities for new employees to connect with their peers and managers. Virtual mentoring programs can also provide support and guidance, helping new hires navigate their roles and the company culture.

Example: Hiring Globally for a Remote-First Company

A fully remote marketing agency based in Europe decided to expand its workforce by hiring talent from around the world. HR professionals faced the challenge of complying with different employment laws and tax regulations in each country. To overcome this, the company partnered with a global Employer of Record (EOR) service that handled local employment contracts, tax withholdings, and benefits administration for employees in multiple countries.

This partnership allowed the company to focus on talent acquisition and management without worrying about the legal complexities of hiring internationally. By adopting a borderless approach to talent acquisition, the company was able to build a diverse and skilled team that brought different perspectives and expertise to the table.

Ensuring Engagement and Productivity Across Time Zones

One of the most significant challenges HR professionals face when managing a borderless workforce is maintaining employee engagement and productivity, especially when employees work in different time zones. Without face-to-face interactions, employees may feel disconnected from their colleagues and the organization, which can lead to decreased motivation and performance.

1. Flexible Work Schedules:

Remote work is built on the premise of flexibility, and this is especially important when managing teams across time zones. HR should encourage a culture of flexibility, where employees can choose their work hours based on their time zone while still meeting organizational objectives. Clear guidelines around availability, core hours for collaboration, and asynchronous work can help teams stay aligned while allowing for flexibility.

2. Fostering Engagement and Inclusion:

Keeping employees engaged and connected when they are geographically dispersed requires consistent effort.

Virtual events, team-building exercises, and regular all-hands meetings can help maintain a sense of community. HR should also prioritize mental health and well-being, as remote workers may face challenges like isolation or burnout. Offering wellness programs, virtual counseling, and fostering an open dialogue around mental health can help mitigate these challenges.

3. Measuring Productivity and Success:

Traditional measures of productivity, such as hours worked or office presence, are no longer applicable in a remote setting. Instead, HR should shift to outcome-based performance management, where success is measured by the quality and impact of work produced. Using key performance indicators (KPIs) and setting clear, achievable goals can provide employees with direction while giving them the autonomy to work on their own schedules. Regular check-ins and performance reviews should focus on results, employee growth, and well-being rather than time spent online.

4. Leveraging Technology to Bridge Time Zones:

Technology plays a pivotal role in maintaining productivity across time zones. HR teams should invest in collaboration tools that facilitate asynchronous work, allowing employees to contribute and communicate at their convenience. Documenting processes, decision making, and updates in shared platforms ensures that everyone stays informed, regardless of when they are working. Moreover, using time zone management tools can help schedule meetings at times that are convenient for all team members, fostering more inclusive communication.

Remote Work Technology and Collaboration Tools

The success of remote work depends significantly on leveraging technology to bridge communication gaps, facilitate seamless collaboration, and ensure effective project management. In a world where employees and teams are increasingly distributed across time zones, HR professionals play a pivotal role in ensuring access to tools that empower productivity and foster connection. This includes deploying video conferencing platforms, cloud-based file-sharing systems, and collaboration software tailored to the organization's needs.

Example: Microsoft Teams for Global Collaboration

A multinational healthcare company operating in Asia, Europe, and North America serves as a prime example of how technology can transform remote work. The company adopted Microsoft Teams as its primary collaboration tool, revolutionizing how employees worked together across regions.

Features and Usage:

Video Meetings: Teams made scheduling and conducting video meetings across time zones effortless, thereby reducing the logistical challenges of global connectivity.

Real-Time File Sharing: The platform enabled employees to share and edit documents collaboratively, eliminating delays in project workflows.

Cross-Departmental Collaboration: Teams fostered collaboration across departments and geographies, helping employees work cohesively toward common goals.

HR's Role in Implementation:

The HR team organized comprehensive training sessions to ensure all employees were well-versed in using Teams' features.

They created user-friendly guides and FAQs, making it easy for employees to troubleshoot common issues and maximize productivity.

Impact and Outcomes

The introduction of Microsoft Teams brought several tangible benefits:

Streamlined Communication: The reliance on email, which had previously caused delays and frequent miscommunication, was significantly reduced. Teams provided a centralized hub for real-time interaction.

Enhanced Productivity: Employees experienced improved efficiency as they could access all necessary tools and information on a single platform.

Stronger Cohesion: Despite being spread across continents, the company cultivated a unified work environment, fostering a sense of inclusion and teamwork.

By prioritizing the right technology and investing in effective training, this healthcare company demonstrated how organizations can successfully adapt to a remote work model while ensuring collaboration, productivity, and employee satisfaction.

Overcoming Cultural Differences in Remote Teams

Managing a borderless workforce also means navigating cultural differences that can impact communication styles, work preferences, and employee expectations. HR professionals must be aware of these differences and implement strategies to bridge cultural gaps, ensuring that employees from diverse backgrounds can collaborate effectively.

Example: Cross-Cultural Training for Remote Teams

A global e-commerce company with a remote workforce spread across Latin America, Europe, and Asia implemented cross-cultural training programs to help employees understand the cultural differences that could affect their interactions with colleagues. The training covered topics such as communication styles, decision-making processes, and work-life balance expectations in different regions.

By providing employees with the tools and knowledge to navigate cultural differences, the HR team fostered a more inclusive and collaborative work environment. Employees were better able to understand and respect each other's perspectives, leading to improved teamwork and fewer misunderstandings.

Remote work and the rise of the borderless workforce have transformed the way organizations operate, offering new opportunities for global collaboration and talent acquisition. However, managing a remote workforce presents its own set of challenges, including ensuring engagement and productivity across different time zones, as well as navigating cultural differences and legal complexities. By implementing strategies such as asynchronous communication, virtual team-building initiatives, and cross-cultural training, HR can effectively manage these challenges.

Professionals can successfully manage remote teams and empower their workforce in a globalized world.

The shift toward remote work has unlocked unprecedented opportunities for organizations to build diverse, global teams. However, managing a borderless workforce requires intentional strategies to foster collaboration, engagement, and productivity. By adopting the right tools and practices, HR leaders can create a thriving virtual work environment where employees feel connected, empowered, and motivated, regardless of their location. The future of work is undoubtedly remote, and the organizations that succeed will be those that embrace the opportunities and challenges of this new global paradigm.

"Mastering talent management across borders ignites global potential, propelling organizations to dominate in a competitive world."

CHAPTER 15

Talent Acquisition and Management Across Borders:

Unlocking Global Potential in a Competitive World

In today's interconnected and highly competitive business environment, the ability to acquire and manage talent across borders has become a critical driver of organizational success. Companies that can successfully navigate the complexities of recruiting and retaining top talent from diverse regions have a distinct advantage in innovation, productivity, and overall performance.

Globalization has expanded the talent pool far beyond local or national borders, offering organizations access to a diverse array of skills, experiences, and cultural perspectives. However, with these opportunities come complex challenges, from navigating different labour markets and regulations to ensuring that talent management practices align with both local and global business needs.

This chapter examines key strategies for harnessing global talent potential, with a focus on global recruitment, international talent mobility, and succession planning within global context. It also explores some real-world examples of how companies are unlocking global potential in a competitive landscape.

Global Recruitment Strategies

Recruiting talent across borders requires organizations to adapt their recruitment strategies to meet the expectations and norms of different regions. HR professionals must navigate diverse legal frameworks, cultural expectations, and varying levels of talent availability while ensuring that the company's global values and goals are maintained.

Example: Regional Adaptation in Recruitment by a Global Tech Firm

A leading global tech firm with operations in Europe, North America, and Asia faced challenges in attracting top talent in emerging markets like India and China, where competition for skilled tech workers is fierce. The company adapted its global recruitment strategy by localizing its employer branding and recruitment practices. In India, for example, the company partnered with leading universities to attract young engineering graduates, offering internships and apprenticeships that created a direct pipeline for full-time employment.

In China, the company focused on social media recruitment, utilizing platforms like WeChat to engage with potential candidates, recognizing that traditional job boards were less effective in the region. This localized approach enabled the company build a strong employer brand and access top-tier talent in competitive markets.

As businesses increasingly seek to expand their global footprint, talent acquisition strategies must evolve to attract top candidates from around the world. Global recruitment requires HR leaders to go beyond traditional sourcing methods and embrace innovative approaches that take into account the diverse labour markets, cultural differences, and competitive landscape.

1. Local Adaptation of Global Strategies:

While having a standardized global recruitment framework ensures consistency, adapting these strategies to local markets is essential for success. Understanding the cultural norms, talent availability, and legal requirements in each country allows organizations to tailor their recruitment efforts. For example, job portals that are popular in one region may be ineffective in another, and hiring expectations ,including job titles, benefits, or negotiation practices, can vary widely.

2. Leveraging Technology for Global Sourcing:

Digital platforms have revolutionized global recruitment, enabling HR teams to reach talent pools that were once inaccessible. LinkedIn, job boards, and AI-powered recruitment platforms allow recruiters to connect with candidates globally. Additionally, technology like AI and Machine Learning can analyze vast amounts of candidate data to match skills with job requirements more efficiently. The key to successful global recruitment lies in leveraging these tools while maintaining a personalized approach to candidate engagement.

3. Employer Branding on a Global Scale:

A strong employer brand that resonates globally is crucial to attracting top talent across borders. Organizations must invest in building a brand that reflects their values, culture, and career opportunities, ensuring that it appeals to diverse audiences. Tailoring messaging to highlight different aspects of the employee value proposition (EVP) that align with local preferences, such as work-life balance in one region or career development opportunities in another, can significant impact in recruitment success.

International Talent Mobility and Relocation

The ability to move talent across borders is essential for companies operating in multiple countries. International talent mobility allows organizations to fill skill gaps, enhance innovation through diverse perspectives, and ensure that leadership talent is distributed across key markets. However, relocation comes with challenges such as navigating immigration laws, managing cultural integration, and ensuring employee satisfaction.

Example: Global Relocation at a Multinational Energy Company

A multinational energy company needed to relocate key talent from its European headquarters to its operations in the Middle East, where a major project required skilled engineers and project managers. To facilitate this, the company's HR team developed a comprehensive talent mobility program that included cultural training, legal support for immigration and work permits, and family assistance programs to help employees and their families adjust to life in a new country.

The company also provided mentoring programs, pairing relocating employees with local managers to ensure a smooth integration into the regional office. By offering robust support throughout the relocation process, the company not only filled critical roles but also retained valuable talent by minimizing the stress associated with moving across borders.

As organizations grow across borders, the need for talent mobility and relocation becomes increasingly essential. Whether it's transferring internal talent to new markets or relocating external hires, effective management of international mobility ensures that the right people are in the right place at the right time, supporting both business goals and employee development.

1. Designing Mobility Programs:

International talent mobility programs must be designed with both organizational needs and employee preferences in mind. Programs should offer flexibility, considering the different motivations for mobility, such as career advancement, personal growth, or life experiences. Additionally, organizations must consider legal and logistical challenges, such as visas, work permits, and tax implications, which vary by country. A well-structured mobility program should also provide support for employees and their families, addressing challenges such as cultural acclimation, housing, and schooling for children.

2. Relocation and Expatriate Support:

Relocating talent internationally requires comprehensive support systems. This includes not only practical relocation services, such as visa assistance, travel, and housing arrangements, but also cultural and language training to help employees adapt to their new environment. Providing a smooth transition is critical to ensuring that employees remain engaged and productive throughout the relocation process. HR leaders should also establish clear repatriation plans, ensuring that employees have opportunities to return to their home countries or explore further international roles as part of their career development.

3. Mobility as a Developmental Tool:

International assignments can serve as valuable opportunities for leadership development and skills enhancement. Organizations should view talent mobility as a way to build global leaders who understand diverse markets, cultures, and business environments. By encouraging cross-border moves and creating pathways for employees to gain international experience, organizations can develop a more agile and globally minded workforce.

Succession Planning in a Global Context

Succession planning in a global organization involves more than identifying future leaders—it requires a deep understanding of regional dynamics, local leadership styles, and cultural nuances. Companies must ensure that their succession plans are flexible enough to accommodate regional differences while fostering a unified leadership pipeline that aligns with global corporate goals.

Example: Cross-Border Succession Planning at a Financial Services Firm

A global financial services firm faced the challenge of ensuring continuity in leadership as it expanded its operations into Latin America and Africa. To address this, the firm's HR team implemented a cross-border succession planning program that identified high-potential leaders in each region and provided them with international leadership development opportunities.

The program included rotational assignments, where emerging leaders were sent to different regional offices to gain a global perspective on the business while building relationships with senior leaders across the company. Additionally, the firm provided leadership training tailored to the cultural contexts of each region, ensuring that future leaders were well-equipped to navigate both local and global challenges.

Succession planning has traditionally focused on identifying and developing future leaders within a single geographical location. However, as businesses expand globally, succession planning must also take a global perspective. HR leaders must ensure that the pipeline of future leaders includes talent from diverse backgrounds and geographies, while aligning succession strategies with the company's global business goals.

1. Building a Global Leadership Pipeline:

A global approach to succession planning involves identifying high-potential talent from across the organization's international footprint. This requires HR to implement talent identification processes that are consistent globally but flexible enough to accommodate local nuances. By developing leadership talent in various regions, organizations can ensure that they have leaders with the necessary cultural and market insights to drive success in different geographies.

2. Developing Cross-Cultural Competencies:

In a global organization, future leaders must be equipped with cross-cultural competencies to manage diverse teams and navigate different markets effectively. Succession planning should focus not only on traditional leadership skills but also on cultural agility, global mindset, and the ability to lead in a matrixed, multicultural environment. Mentoring, coaching, and international assignments can all play a role in developing these competencies.

3. Aligning Succession with Business Strategy:

Succession planning should be closely aligned with the organization's long-term business strategy. As companies enter new markets or expand their global operations, succession plans must be adjusted to ensure that the right talent is in place to support these initiatives. This may involve identifying talent who are not only ready to step into leadership roles but also capable of driving global growth, innovation, and change management.

Cultural Considerations in Talent Acquisition and Management

Cultural differences play a significant role in how talent acquisition and management strategies are implemented across borders. HR professionals must understand the cultural norms that influence communication, decision-making, and employee expectations to ensure that their strategies are effective in diverse regions.

Example: Adapting Leadership Styles in Asia

An European company expanding its operations into Japan and South Korea struggled initially with talent retention and employee engagement. After conducting an internal review, the company realized that its leadership style, which emphasized individual performance and direct feedback, was not resonating with employees in these countries, where group harmony and indirect communication are highly valued.

To address this, the company's HR team adapted its leadership development programs to reflect local cultural expectations. Managers received training on how to deliver feedback in a more nuanced and respectful manner, and the company introduced more team-based performance evaluations to align with the collectivist values of the region. These changes helped improve employee engagement and retention, demonstrating the importance of cultural adaptability in global talent management.

Technology's Role in Cross-Border Talent Acquisition

Technology has played a transformative role in enabling companies to recruit and manage talent across borders. From AI-driven recruitment platforms to virtual onboarding systems, technology allows organizations to streamline their talent acquisition processes, expand their talent pool, and enhance the overall candidate experience.

Example: AI-Powered Recruitment at a Global E-Commerce Company

A global e-commerce company, seeking to scale its operations rapidly across multiple regions, implemented an AI-powered recruitment platform to manage its high-volume hiring needs. The platform used machine learning algorithms to screen resumes, assess candidates based on predefined criteria, and predict which candidates were most likely to succeed in the company's fast-paced environment.

The use of AI not only reduced the time spent on initial screening but also helped the company identify qualified candidates who may have been overlooked in a manual process. By integrating the AI platform with its global HR system, the company was able to create a more efficient and consistent recruitment process across all of its regions.

Challenges and Opportunities in Managing Cross-Border Talent

While global talent acquisition offers significant advantages, it also presents challenges, such as navigating different employment laws, managing compensation and benefits across regions, and ensuring that employees feel connected to the company's global mission. Organizations must comply with a complex web of regulations, including tax implications, visa requirements, and labour laws, which vary widely across countries. Even slight missteps in these areas can result in legal penalties, reputational damage, or disruptions in operations.

Cultural differences add another layer of complexity, as employees from diverse backgrounds may have varying expectations regarding leadership styles, decision-making processes, and work-life balance. Misaligned integration efforts can result in communication breakdowns, disengagement, or tension among team members. Employers must also consider time zone differences, which can impact collaboration and create challenges in maintaining productivity and fostering a sense of inclusion for distributed teams.

At the same time, these challenges present unique opportunities. Organizations that embrace cultural diversity can foster innovation through fresh perspectives and varied problem-solving approaches. Building a global workforce also provides access to specialized skills that may be scarce in the company's home market. By investing in tools such as collaborative technology, virtual engagement strategies, and cultural training programs, businesses can transform these challenges into stepping stones for sustainable growth. Companies that succeed in creating inclusive, equitable, and globally aware workplaces are better positioned to thrive in an interconnected world, attracting top talent and establishing themselves as leaders in their industries.

Example: Navigating Compensation Differences in Global Markets

A global pharmaceutical company faced challenges in aligning its compensation and benefits packages across different regions. In North America and Europe, the company offered competitive salaries and comprehensive health benefits; however in emerging markets such as Southeast Asia and Africa, local compensation norms and expectations differed. To address this, the company's HR team conducted market research to understand the compensation expectations in each region and adapted its packages accordingly.

In some regions, offering flexible work arrangements and opportunities for professional development was more attractive to employees than higher salaries. By tailoring its compensation and benefits strategy to the needs of each region, the company was able to attract and retain top talent while maintaining global consistency in its HR practices.

Talent acquisition and management across borders is crucial for organizations striving to thrive in today's competitive and interconnected world. With the rise of globalization, businesses must adapt their recruitment strategies to align with local realities, such as cultural nuances, regional labour laws, and market-specific talent demands. Simultaneously, they must navigate the complexities of international talent mobility, ensuring that employees can seamlessly transition across borders while maintaining engagement and productivity. Developing succession plans that balance global priorities with regional needs is equally essential, as it allows organizations to build a resilient leadership pipeline that can operate effectively across diverse markets.

By fostering diversity, promoting cross-cultural collaboration, and cultivating globally minded leaders, companies can create a workforce that is not only capable but also highly innovative and adaptable. By leveraging advanced technology and cultural insights, HR professionals can streamline processes, enhance decision-making, and effectively address the unique challenges of managing talent across borders. Organizations that adopt these strategies will be well-positioned to transform cross-border complexities into opportunities, driving growth, innovation, and long-term competitive advantage in the rapid evolving world of global talent management.

"Effective cross-cultural communication bridges divides, strengthens collaboration, and drives success in the global workforce."

Chapter 16

Cross-Cultural Communication in Global HR :

Bridging Gaps to Foster Global Collaboration

In today's globalized workplace, effective cross-cultural communication is critical for HR professionals as they manage diverse teams spread across multiple countries. With employees coming from diverse cultural backgrounds, communication styles can vary significantly, and differences in language, non-verbal cues, and cultural norms can lead to misunderstandings, reduce efficiency, and foster conflict if not properly managed.

Cross-cultural communication plays a key role in fostering global collaboration, ensuring that employees understand each other and work effectively despite cultural differences. As businesses expand across borders and teams become more diverse, effective cross-cultural communication has become a cornerstone of global HR practices.

This chapter examines strategies for overcoming language barriers, understanding non-verbal communication across cultures, and developing cultural intelligence in HR professionals. It provides real-world examples of how organizations have successfully bridged cultural gaps, communication gaps, fostered collaboration, and built culturally aware teams in a globalized world.

Overcoming Language Barriers in Multinational Teams

Language barriers are one of the most common challenges in cross-cultural communication, particularly in multinational organizations where employees speak different native languages. While English is often the common language in global companies, employees who are non-native speakers may struggle with fluency, leading to miscommunication and misunderstandings.

Example: Language Training in a Global Pharmaceutical Company

A global pharmaceutical company with employees across Europe and Asia faced communication challenges as team members in Germany and Japan struggled to communicate fluently in English. To address this, the company's HR team introduced language training programs, offering English lessons for employees in non-English speaking regions and cultural language classes for employees who frequently collaborated with teams in Japan and China.

Additionally, the company provided language assistance tools, such as translation apps and access to bilingual HR support staff, to help employees overcome language barriers in meetings and daily communication. This investment in language training improved collaboration across the company's international teams, reduced misunderstandings, and fostered a more inclusive work environment.

Language is often the most obvious barrier in global communication. In multinational teams, individuals may speak different native languages, and even if a common corporate language (usually English) is adopted, varying levels of proficiency can impact clarity and effectiveness. HR professionals play a key role in ensuring that language differences do not hinder communication or teamwork.

1. Implementing a Common Language Policy:

While encouraging a shared corporate language is important for cohesive communication, it's equally critical to recognize that not all employees will have the same level of fluency. HR can provide language training for team members to enhance their proficiency and confidence in using the common language, which promotes better collaboration. Additionally, using clear and straightforward language in corporate communications can minimize misunderstandings.

2. Utilizing Translation and Interpretation Tools:

Technology can be a great enabler in overcoming language barriers. Tools like real-time translation apps, multilingual email templates, and AI-powered communication platforms can help bridge language and cultural gaps in understanding. HR can also support the use of professional interpreters during important meetings or negotiations when precision is key.

3. Fostering Inclusivity for Non-Native Speakers:

It's essential to create a culture where non-native speakers feel comfortable contributing without fear of judgment. This involves HR encouraging patience among native speakers, slowing down conversations, and ensuring that non-native speakers have the opportunity to clarify points they don't understand. Providing written summaries or follow-ups after verbal meetings can also help reinforce understanding.

Nonverbal Communication Across Cultures

While language is an essential aspect of communication, non-verbal cues such as body language, facial expressions, and gestures also play a significant role in how messages are interpreted. Non-verbal communication differs significantly across cultures, and HR professionals must be aware of these differences to avoid potential misinterpretations.

Example: Non-Verbal Communication in Japan vs. the United States

In Japan, non-verbal cues convey respect, politeness, and agreement indirectly. Silence can indicate contemplation or agreement, while in the United States, it may suggest a lack of engagement or understanding. Similarly, direct eye contact in Japan can seem confrontational, whereas in the U.S., it signals confidence and honesty.

A global consulting firm with teams in both Japan and the United States encountered these differences in non-verbal communication, leading to confusion during virtual meetings. The HR team implemented cross-cultural communication training, educating employees on these differences and teaching them how to interpret non-verbal cues in various cultural contexts. This helped improve collaboration and reduced frustration caused by misinterpreting non-verbal signals.

Non-verbal cues—such as gestures, facial expressions, and body language—vary significantly across cultures. What may be considered an appropriate form of non-verbal communication in one country could be perceived as offensive or confusing in another. Understanding these nuances is critical for HR professionals working with global teams.

1. Cultural Sensitivity to Non-Verbal Cues:

HR leaders should be aware of key differences in non-verbal communication. For instance, eye contact is interpreted differently across cultures—while it may be seen as a sign of confidence in Western cultures, it can be considered disrespectful or aggressive in some Asian cultures. Similarly, gestures like handshakes, nodding, or the use of personal space can have varied meanings.

2. Training Teams on Non-Verbal Differences:

Providing cultural sensitivity training to employees can enhance awareness of non-verbal differences, thereby reducing the risk of misunderstandings. Workshops or role-playing exercises can be effective ways to demonstrate how different cultures interpret body language and gestures. This also helps build empathy and cultural appreciation within the team.

3. Adapting to Virtual Communication:

In remote work environments, non-verbal communication can be limited to facial expressions and tone of voice during video calls. HR should ensure that team members are aware of these constraints and encourage clarity in verbal communication to compensate for the reduced use of body language.

Developing Cultural Intelligence in HR Professionals

Cultural intelligence, or CQ, refers to an individual's ability to understand and adapt to cultural differences in communication, behaviour, and work styles. HR professionals need to develop high levels of cultural intelligence to navigate the complexities of managing a global workforce. By fostering cultural intelligence, HR teams can create a more inclusive environment and improve cross-cultural collaboration.

Example: Cultural Intelligence in a Multinational Tech Company

A multinational tech company with employees in North America, Europe, and Asia implemented a cultural intelligence development program for its HR professionals.

The program included workshops on cultural awareness, cross-cultural conflict resolution, and communication strategies tailored to different regions. HR teams were also encouraged to participate in global exchange programs, where they spent time working in different regional offices to gain first-hand experience with local cultural norms.

This investment in cultural intelligence allowed the HR team to better understand the unique needs of employees in each region and to develop HR policies that were culturally sensitive. As a result, the company saw improved employee engagement and a reduction in cross-cultural conflicts, as HR was able to mediate and resolve issues more effectively.

Cultural intelligence (CQ) refers to the ability to understand and adapt to cultural differences, which is increasingly important for HR professionals managing global workforces. High cultural intelligence enables HR leaders to navigate complex intercultural interactions, resolve conflicts, and create inclusive policies that consider the needs of diverse employees.

1. Building Awareness and Knowledge:

Cultural intelligence begins with awareness—understanding that cultural differences exist and recognizing their impact on communication and behavior. HR professionals must actively seek knowledge about the cultures represented in their workforce. This can include learning about local customs, values, and communication styles through research, training, or first-hand experience.

2. Developing Cross-Cultural Skills:

In addition to knowledge, HR leaders must develop the skills to navigate cross-cultural interactions effectively. This includes being open-minded, empathetic, and adaptable in different cultural settings. HR should also promote these skills across the organization, encouraging managers and employees to engage in cultural intelligence development through training programs, mentorship, and international exposure.

3. Embedding Cultural Intelligence in HR Practices:

Cultural intelligence should not be limited to individual learning but embedded in organizational policies and practices. This can include tailoring performance management systems to account for cultural differences, ensuring that recruitment processes are free from cultural bias, and designing benefits programs that reflect the values and needs of a diverse workforce.

Strategies for Effective Cross-Cultural Negotiations and Conflict Resolution

Negotiation styles and approaches to conflict resolution vary across cultures, and HR professionals must be adept at managing these differences. In some cultures, direct confrontation is acceptable and even encouraged, while in others, conflict is avoided at all costs, and issues are resolved through indirect communication. Understanding these cultural nuances is essential for HR professionals involved in negotiations and conflict resolution across borders.

Example: Conflict Resolution in a Middle Eastern Construction Firm

A construction firm based in the Middle East had a diverse workforce with employees from South Asia, Europe, and the Middle East. Conflict arose between teams due to differing approaches to project management and communication styles. European employees preferred direct, face-to-face discussions to address issues, while employees from South Asia were more accustomed to resolving conflicts through intermediaries or indirect communication.

The HR team introduced conflict resolution training that focused on understanding cultural differences in negotiation styles. They also appointed culturally aware mediators who could facilitate discussions between teams and help bridge the gap between direct and indirect communication preferences. This strategy helped reduce workplace tensions and enabled the teams to work more collaboratively on shared goals. In a global workplace, conflicts can arise due to cultural misunderstandings or differing communication styles. HR plays a pivotal role in facilitating cross-cultural negotiations and resolving disputes in a way that respects the diverse perspectives of all parties involved.

1. Understanding Cultural Approaches to Conflict:

Different cultures have varying approaches to conflict—some may prefer direct confrontation, while others might avoid it in favor of preserving harmony. HR professionals must understand these cultural tendencies to effectively mediate disputes. For example, in many Western cultures, open dialogue and debate are encouraged, whereas in East Asian cultures, conflict may be handled more subtly or privately to save face.

2. Adapting Negotiation Styles to Cultural Contexts:

Negotiation styles also differ across cultures. In some cultures, negotiations are viewed as competitive, with a focus on winning, while in others, the emphasis is on building long-term relationships and mutual benefit. HR professionals can facilitate better negotiations by aligning their strategies with the cultural expectations of the participants. This might involve adjusting communication styles, being patient with the decision-making process, or recognizing the importance of personal relationships in some cultures.

3. Mediation and Conflict Resolution:

HR should act as a neutral mediator in cross-cultural conflicts, ensuring that both parties feel heard and respected. Effective conflict resolution requires active listening, cultural sensitivity, and finding common ground. HR can also create structured frameworks for conflict resolution that consider cultural differences, such as incorporating elements of restorative justice or involving third-party mediators when necessary.

Cross-cultural communication is a cornerstone of managing and empowering a global workforce in today's interconnected world. With employees coming from diverse backgrounds, effective communication is critical to fostering collaboration, inclusivity, and innovation. HR professionals play a pivotal role in bridging communication gaps, addressing language barriers, and navigating cultural differences, particularly in areas such as negotiation, decision-making, and conflict resolution. By actively fostering cultural intelligence and promoting an understanding of diverse communication styles, HR can cultivate an environment where employees feel valued and respected, regardless of their cultural background.

Organizations that prioritize cross-cultural communication can build stronger, more cohesive teams that leverage their diversity for greater creativity and problem-solving. Providing employees with training and resources to navigate cross-cultural interactions equips them with the tools needed to communicate effectively and work collaboratively across borders. This not only enhances day-to-day interactions but also builds trust and strengthens relationships within global teams. By fostering mutual respect and a shared sense of purpose, organizations unlock the full potential of their workforce, enabling them to adapt to new challenges and achieve long-term success in an increasingly competitive and globalized market.

"HR is the catalyst for cultural integration during mergers and acquisitions, ensuring seamless synergy that drives organizational strength and success."

Chapter 17

HR's Role in Managing Cultural Integration During Mergers and Acquisitions:

Harmonizing Cultures for Seamless Organizational Synergy

Mergers and acquisitions (M&As) are often pursued to achieve strategic growth, expand market reach, or increase operational efficiency. However, beyond financial and operational considerations, one of the most critical and complex aspects of M&As is the integration of corporate cultures. HR plays a pivotal role in this process, ensuring that the blending of cultures leads to a harmonious, unified organization rather than a clash that derails the merger's potential benefits.

Mergers and acquisitions (M&A) are not just about financial transactions and operational integration. One of the most critical, yet often overlooked, aspects of M&A success is the integration of organizational cultures. HR plays a pivotal role in harmonizing cultures, ensuring that both companies align their values, work practices, and employee expectations to create a unified, high-performing organization. Without effective cultural integration, even the most strategically sound mergers can falter.

In this chapter, we will examine how HR can evaluate cultural fit, devise strategies to integrate cultures, and draw lessons from real-world examples of successful and unsuccessful integrations. This chapter also explores the HR strategies and tools needed to manage cultural integration during M&As.

Due Diligence: Assessing Cultural Fit Pre-Merger

Assessing cultural compatibility before a merger is as important as evaluating financial or operational synergies. HR professionals must perform cultural due diligence to identify potential areas of friction between the merging organizations. This involves understanding the corporate cultures, values, communication styles, and leadership approaches of both companies. Before a merger or acquisition is finalized, it's crucial to assess not only the financial and operational aspects of the deal but also the cultural fit between the two organizations. Cultural misalignment is a leading cause of post-merger failure, so HR must take a proactive role in conducting cultural due diligence.

1. Evaluating Corporate Values and Beliefs:

HR's due diligence should begin with an assessment of each organization's values, beliefs, and norms. Are both companies aligned in their approach to employee engagement, leadership style, decision-making processes, and risk tolerance? Identifying areas of alignment and divergence can help predict potential cultural clashes post-merger.

2. Employee Sentiment and Work Environment:

HR should also gauge employee sentiment and the overall work environment in both organizations. This can be done through surveys, interviews, and observation of day-to-day practices. For example, one company may have a highly hierarchical structure with strict decision-making protocols, while the other may promote decentralized decision-making and employee empowerment. Understanding these dynamics is key to determining how the two cultures will interact.

3. Leadership Compatibility:

Another critical area for HR to assess is the compatibility of leadership teams. Leaders set the tone for the organization's culture, and conflicting leadership styles can create confusion and disruption during integration. HR must evaluate how well the leadership teams can work together, their openness to change, and their ability to lead in a post-merger environment.

Example: Cultural Assessment in a Tech Acquisition

A global technology firm acquired a start-up known for its innovation and agility. The acquiring company had a more traditional, hierarchical culture, while the start-up had a flat organizational structure with a strong emphasis on employee empowerment and rapid decision-making. During the due diligence phase, HR identified this cultural difference as a potential challenge and recommended implementing cross-functional teams to foster collaboration between the two entities. By acknowledging the cultural differences upfront, HR was able to design a cultural integration strategy that leveraged the strengths of both organizations while minimizing friction.

Strategies for Blending Diverse Corporate Cultures

Once a merger or acquisition is finalized, the real work of integrating cultures begins. HR must lead the effort to blend diverse corporate cultures in a way that maintains employee morale, preserves key talent, and aligns the new organization with its strategic goals. Some strategies for successful cultural integration include:

1. Creating a Shared Vision and Values

HR should work with leadership teams from both organizations to create a shared vision and set of values that employees can rally around. This shared vision serves as the foundation for the new culture and helps employees understand how their roles contribute to the success of the newly merged company.

2. Open Communication and Transparent Leadership

Transparency is critical during cultural integration. Employees may feel uncertain or resistant to change, and it is HR's responsibility to facilitate open communication channels where employees can voice their concerns and receive updates on the integration process. Leaders from both organizations should be visible and engaged, demonstrating a commitment to blending the cultures.

Example: Cultural Integration in a Healthcare Merger

When two major healthcare organizations merged, HR played a key role in aligning the cultures of the two companies, which had very different approaches to patient care and employee management. One company emphasized personalized, patient-centered care, while the other was focused on operational efficiency and standardization. HR facilitated workshops and town hall meetings where employees from both organizations could share their concerns and suggestions for integrating these approaches.

By promoting open dialogue and creating a shared vision that combined the strengths of both organizations, HR was able to foster a culture that balanced patient care with operational efficiency. As a result, the merged organization saw increased employee engagement and improved patient outcomes.

Once the merger or acquisition is complete, HR must take the lead in creating a strategy to blend the two cultures into a cohesive whole. This requires careful planning, clear communication, and a focus on building a shared identity that reflects the best elements of both organizations.

1. Establishing a Unified Vision:

The first step in cultural integration is to establish a unified vision that resonates with employees from both organizations. This vision should encapsulate the strategic goals of the merger, while also reflecting shared values that can serve as the foundation for the new, integrated culture. HR should facilitate workshops and discussions to co-create this vision with leadership and employees, ensuring that it feels authentic and inclusive.

2. Communication and Transparency:

Open and transparent communication is essential to easing the uncertainty that often accompanies M&As. HR should regularly communicate updates about the integration process, providing employees with clarity on how the merger will impact them and the organization as a whole. Additionally, leaders should be encouraged to openly discuss the cultural challenges they foresee and the steps being taken to address them.

3. Cultural Champions and Integration Teams:

One effective strategy for blending cultures is to establish integration teams composed of employees from both organizations. These teams can serve as cultural champions, modelling the behaviours and attitudes that support the new, unified culture. HR should also provide training on cultural sensitivity and change management to help these teams lead by example and address any cultural friction that arises.

4. Celebrating Wins from Both Cultures:

Rather than imposing one culture over the other, HR should strive to create a new culture that celebrates the strengths of both legacy organizations. This can be done by recognizing and preserving traditions, rituals, and practices that employees value. For example, if one company has a strong tradition of celebrating employee milestones, this practice can be adopted by the new entity to foster continuity and employee engagement.

Managing Leadership Styles and Employee Expectations

Leadership styles often differ significantly between merging companies, and these differences can create tension during integration. HR must identify leadership disparities early and develop strategies to harmonize leadership approaches, ensuring that employees receive consistent messaging and guidance from their leaders.

Example: Leadership Integration in a Global Bank Merger

When two global banks, JPMorgan Chase and Bank One, merged in 2004, HR discovered that the leadership styles in the two companies were markedly different. One bank had a top-down, directive leadership approach, while the other embraced a more collaborative, consensus-driven model. To address this, HR designed a leadership alignment program that involved leadership workshops, coaching sessions, and joint leadership retreats. These initiatives helped leaders from both banks adopt a more unified approach to decision-making and communication, which eased the cultural integration process and improved employee confidence in the new leadership team.

Retaining Talent During Cultural Integration

One of the most significant risks during an M&A is the loss of key talent. Employees may feel uncertain about their future in the newly merged organization and decide to leave. HR must proactively manage this risk by providing clarity, addressing concerns, and ensuring that top talent feels valued and secure in their roles.

Example: Talent Retention in a Retail Merger

In a merger between two retail giants, HR faced the challenge of retaining high-performing employees, particularly at the managerial level. The fear of job redundancies and changes in company culture led to increased turnover. To address this, HR launched a talent retention program that identified key talent across both organizations and offered retention bonuses, career development opportunities, and mentoring programs to ensure these employees remained engaged during the integration process. By providing clear communication about their roles and career paths in the merged organization, HR was able to retain most of the company's top talent.

Case Studies of Successful and Failed Cultural Integrations in M&As

Examining real-world examples of cultural integration during mergers and acquisitions provides valuable lessons on what works and what doesn't. Below, we explore a few notable cases of both successful and failed cultural integrations.

1. Successful Integrations:

Disney's Acquisition of Pixar

When Disney acquired Pixar in 2006, many industry analysts were concerned that Disney's more traditional corporate culture would clash with Pixar's creative, free-spirited environment. However, the merger was a success, mainly due to Disney's willingness to preserve Pixar's unique culture. Disney allowed Pixar to maintain its own identity and operational autonomy, while leveraging its resources to enhance Pixar's growth. This approach of respecting and valuing the acquired company's culture, rather than trying to impose change, resulted in a seamless integration that strengthened both organizations.

Daimler and Chrysler

The merger between Daimler-Benz and Chrysler in 1998 is often highlighted as a failure, but in recent years, the integration has seen a resurgence. Early on, the companies struggled due to significant cultural differences—Daimler's Germanic, hierarchical culture clashed with Chrysler's more informal, American approach. However, after the initial failure, HR leaders on both sides worked to foster better cross-cultural understanding through leadership development, shared goals, and collaborative projects. Today, the companies operate with a better sense of unity, though it took years to achieve this alignment.

2. Failed Integration:

AOL and Time Warner

The merger between AOL and Time Warner in 2000 is often cited as one of the most disastrous in corporate history, and cultural misalignment was a significant factor in its failure. The two companies had starkly different cultures—AOL was a fast-moving tech company, while Time Warner was a traditional media giant with bureaucratic processes. HR leaders have failed to bridge the gap between these two cultures, resulting in confusion, infighting, and a lack of shared purpose. Employees felt disconnected from the new organization, and the merger ultimately unravelled.

Cultural integration is a critical factor in determining the success or failure of mergers and acquisitions. By conducting thorough cultural due diligence, developing thoughtful strategies to blend cultures, and learning from past experiences, HR professionals can play a crucial role in ensuring that M&As lead to seamless organizational synergy. The key to successful integration lies in valuing and respecting the unique elements of each culture while building a shared vision for the future—one that employees across both organizations can rally around as they move forward together.

HR plays a vital role in managing cultural integration during mergers and acquisitions. By conducting cultural due diligence, facilitating open communication, aligning leadership styles, and retaining key talent, HR professionals can help ensure a seamless organizational synergy. Successful cultural integration requires a deep understanding of both companies' values, work practices, and employee expectations, and HR must take a proactive approach to harmonizing these elements to drive long-term success.

PART III:
Future Trends and Challenges

"HR in the era of blockchain and digital credentials empowers trust and transparency, revolutionizing the future of work with unparalleled integrity and efficiency."

CHAPTER 18

HR in the Era of Blockchain and Digital Credentials:

Empowering Trust and Transparency

As technology continues to reshape the landscape of Human Resources, blockchain and digital credentials have emerged as transformative forces. Blockchain technology, known for its secure and transparent nature, offers HR professionals new ways to manage employee data, verify credentials, and streamline recruitment processes.

This chapter examines how HR can leverage blockchain and digital credentials to empower trust and transparency within organizations, providing examples and case studies that illustrate the practical applications of these technologies.

Understanding Blockchain Technology

Blockchain is a decentralized digital ledger that records transactions across multiple computers in such a way that the registered transactions cannot be altered retroactively.

This technology offers a high level of security, transparency, and traceability, making it an ideal solution for HR applications, particularly in areas such as recruitment, credential verification, and employee data management.

Security and Trust:

Blockchain's immutable nature ensures that once data is recorded, it cannot be changed, thus enhancing trust in the information.

Transparency:

All stakeholders have access to the same information, reducing discrepancies and fostering a culture of transparency.

Efficiency:

Automating processes such as background checks and qualification verification can significantly reduce the time and resources spent on these tasks.

The Role of HR in Implementing Blockchain Solutions

HR professionals must understand how to implement blockchain technology within their organizations effectively. This involves:

Identifying Use Cases:

Determining where blockchain can add value, such as in recruitment, employee records management, and compliance.

Engaging Stakeholders:

Collaborating with IT departments and blockchain experts to develop and integrate blockchain solutions that align with HR needs.

Training Employees:

Providing training and resources for HR staff to understand blockchain technology and its implications for their work.

Blockchain Applications in HR

Blockchain technology can be applied in various HR functions, including:

1. Credential Verification

Example: HireRight's Blockchain Verification Service

HireRight, a background screening company, has begun using blockchain technology to enhance the verification of educational and professional credentials. By partnering with academic institutions and employers, HireRight creates a secure blockchain network where verified credentials can be stored and accessed by employers during the recruitment process.

This system not only speeds up the verification process but also reduces the risk of fraud, as employers can easily confirm the authenticity of a candidate's qualifications without relying on third-party verification services.

2. Recruitment and Talent Acquisition

Case Study: IBM and the Use of Blockchain in Hiring

IBM has been at the forefront of implementing blockchain in HR, particularly in recruitment. The company has developed a blockchain platform that enables candidates to securely store their resumes and credentials. When applying for jobs, candidates can grant prospective employers access to their verified credentials through the blockchain.

This approach streamlines the hiring process, as HR professionals can instantly access verified information about candidates, reducing the time spent on background checks and increasing the quality of hires.

3. Employee Data Management

Example: The Use of Blockchain for Secure Employee Records

Organizations are exploring blockchain solutions to manage employee records securely. By creating a decentralized database of employee information, organizations can ensure that sensitive data is protected from breaches while allowing authorized parties to access it seamlessly.

For instance, a multinational corporation implemented a blockchain-based HR management system to store employee data securely across its global offices. This system not only enhanced data security but also ensured compliance with data privacy regulations, as employees could control who accessed their information.

Digital Credentials and Their Impact on HR

Digital credentials represent verified qualifications, certifications, and achievements that can be securely shared and verified through digital platforms. They provide a modern alternative to traditional paper-based credentials, enabling HR professionals to assess candidates' qualifications quickly and efficiently.

1. Verifiable Digital Badges

Example: Credly's Digital Badges

Credly, a digital credentialing platform, allows organizations to issue digital badges to employees who have completed specific training programs or achieved certain skills. These badges can be easily shared on professional networks, such as LinkedIn, allowing employees to showcase their accomplishments to potential employers.

By adopting digital badges, organizations enhance employee engagement and motivation while providing a verifiable method for candidates to demonstrate their qualifications in the job market.

2. Enhancing the Hiring Process

Case Study: Purdue University's Digital Credential Initiative

Purdue University has launched an initiative to issue digital credentials to its graduates, enabling them to easily share their verified achievements with employers. By using blockchain technology to verify and store these credentials, Purdue enhances the credibility of its graduates in the job market.

Employers can access a secure database to verify candidates' credentials instantly, reducing the time spent on background checks and ensuring that they are hiring qualified individuals.

Challenges and Considerations in Implementing Blockchain in HR

While blockchain and digital credentials offer significant benefits to HR, there are challenges that organizations must consider:

Integration with Existing Systems:

Implementing blockchain solutions requires integration with existing HR systems and processes. Organizations may face technical challenges in aligning these systems effectively.

Regulatory Compliance:

HR professionals must ensure that blockchain implementations comply with data protection regulations, particularly concerning employee data privacy.

Cultural Resistance:

Employees may be resistant to adopting new technologies, and HR must provide adequate training and support to facilitate a smooth transition.

Scalability:

As organizations grow, ensuring that blockchain solutions can scale to meet increasing demands is essential. HR must work with IT departments to evaluate the scalability of proposed solutions.

Future Trends in HR and Blockchain

The future of HR will likely see increased adoption of blockchain technology and digital credentials as organizations seek to enhance trust, transparency, and efficiency. Key trends to watch include:

Wider Adoption of Blockchain for Verification:

As more organizations recognize the benefits of blockchain for credential verification, its use will expand beyond tech companies to various industries, including healthcare, finance, and education.

Integration with Artificial Intelligence:

The combination of blockchain and AI could enhance recruitment processes by automating credential verification and candidate assessment, allowing HR professionals to focus on strategic decision-making.

Collaborative Platforms:

Emerging platforms that combine blockchain with collaborative tools will enable organizations to share and verify credentials across industries, fostering greater transparency and trust in the job market.

Blockchain technology and digital credentials are driving a paradigm shift in the way human resources (HR) functions, fundamentally transforming talent management processes by fostering trust, transparency, and efficiency. The adoption of blockchain solutions is enabling organizations to enhance operations in multiple areas, including credential verification, employee data management, and recruitment. By leveraging the decentralized and immutable nature of blockchain, HR departments can streamline traditionally cumbersome processes, such as verifying educational qualifications, certifications, and work histories, which often require significant time and manual effort. This technology reduces the risk of fraudulent claims by ensuring that all credentials are authentic, verified, and tamper-proof, thus building confidence in the hiring process.

Furthermore, blockchain-based systems provide secure and transparent platforms for storing employee data, granting access only to authorized parties. This not only safeguards sensitive information but also ensures compliance with data protection regulations, which is a growing concern in today's digital landscape. In recruitment, blockchain facilitates a more seamless and efficient experience by offering real-time access to verified candidate profiles, enabling recruiters to make faster, more informed decisions.

As organizations around the world continue to embrace these innovations, the role of HR is becoming increasingly strategic. HR professionals are now tasked with not just adopting these technologies but also aligning them with the organization's goals to maximize their impact. This includes ensuring that the workforce is equipped with verified skills and qualifications tailored to meet the evolving demands of a dynamic and competitive job market. By bridging the gap between technology and talent, HR will play a pivotal role in shaping the future of work, driving organizational growth, and fostering a culture of innovation in an ever-changing global economy.

"HR is the cornerstone during economic downturns, guiding organizations through crises with strength, adaptability, and strategic foresight."

Chapter 19

The Role of HR in Navigating Economic Downturns and Crisis Management:

Steering Organizations Through Stormy Waters

Economic downturns and crises can have profound impacts on organizations and their employees. The COVID-19 pandemic, the 2008 financial crisis, and various regional recessions have underscored the importance of effective crisis management and the pivotal role that Human Resources (HR) plays in steering organizations through turbulent times. HR professionals are not only responsible for maintaining compliance with legal and regulatory requirements but also for ensuring employee well-being, morale, and engagement during challenging periods.

This chapter examines the critical role of HR in navigating economic downturns, featuring real-world examples and case studies that demonstrate best practices in crisis management.

Understanding the Crisis: Identifying the Challenges

During an economic downturn, organizations face a multitude of challenges, including:

Financial Constraints:

Reduced revenue can lead to budget cuts, which in turn can impact employee salaries, benefits, and the resources available for training and development.

Employee Morale:

Economic uncertainty often leads to anxiety among employees, affecting their productivity and engagement levels.

Workforce Reduction:

Organizations may need to consider layoffs, furloughs, or restructuring to adapt to the new economic reality, creating additional stress for both management and employees.

Talent Retention:

The risk of losing key talent during a downturn can have long-term implications for an organization's recovery and growth.

Adaptation to Change:

Organizations must pivot quickly to adapt to changing market conditions, requiring agility and innovative thinking from their workforce.

HR's Role in Crisis Management

HR professionals are uniquely positioned to address these challenges through strategic planning and effective communication. Here are some of the key roles HR plays in crisis management:

1. Communication and Transparency:

Open and honest communication is crucial during times of crisis. HR must ensure that employees receive timely information about the organization's status, changes in policies, and any potential impacts on their roles.

Example: Marriott International during COVID-19

When the COVID-19 pandemic struck, Marriott International faced significant revenue losses due to travel restrictions. The HR team implemented a robust communication strategy, keeping employees informed about the evolving situation and the company's response. Regular updates via emails, virtual town halls, and a dedicated COVID-19 resource hub on the intranet helped maintain transparency and build trust among employees.

2. Employee Support and Well-being:

Providing support to employees during a crisis is vital for maintaining morale and productivity. HR should implement programs that focus on mental health, stress management, and overall well-being.

Case Study: Unilever's Mental Health Initiatives

Unilever proactively addressed employee well-being during the pandemic by offering mental health resources, including virtual counseling, mindfulness sessions, and flexible work arrangements. The HR team recognized that employees were facing unprecedented challenges, and by prioritizing their mental health, Unilever not only supported its workforce but also maintained engagement levels during a difficult period.

3.Talent Management and Retention:

During a crisis, retaining top talent is critical for organizational recovery. HR must identify high-potential employees and implement strategies to keep them engaged and motivated.

Example: Salesforce's Talent Retention Strategy

Salesforce, a leading cloud-based software company, implemented a talent retention strategy during the 2008 financial crisis that focused on employee development and engagement. Rather than resorting to layoffs, the company opted to invest in its employees through training programs and development opportunities. This approach helped retain top talent, positioning Salesforce for growth once the economy rebounded.

4. Flexibility and Adaptability:

HR must foster a culture of flexibility and adaptability within the organization. This includes promoting remote work, flexible schedules, and innovative solutions to maintain productivity during challenging times.

Case Study: Google's Flexible Work Policy

During the COVID-19 pandemic, Google quickly transitioned to remote work for its employees. The HR team introduced flexible work policies, allowing employees to choose their working hours and providing resources to set up home offices. By empowering employees with flexibility, Google maintained productivity and employee satisfaction during a time of uncertainty.

Developing Crisis Management Plans

To successfully navigate the challenges of economic downturns, HR must create robust and comprehensive crisis management plans that serve as a roadmap for the organization's response strategies. These plans should be tailored to address the unique needs of the organization while providing a framework for maintaining stability, ensuring transparency, and supporting employees through uncertain times. The key components of an effective crisis management plan include the following:

1. Risk Assessment

The first step in crisis planning involves identifying potential risks and challenges that the organization may encounter during an economic downturn. These risks may include financial constraints, declining employee morale, and shifting market conditions. By conducting a thorough assessment, HR can anticipate potential impacts and develop proactive strategies to mitigate them, ensuring that the organization is prepared to respond effectively.

2. Crisis Communication Protocols

Clear and consistent communication is critical during a crisis. HR must establish communication protocols and channels to disseminate information to employees in a timely and transparent manner. This includes outlining who will deliver key messages, how information will be shared, and ensuring that employees feel informed and supported throughout the crisis.

3. Employee Support Programs

Supporting employees during times of uncertainty is essential to maintaining morale and engagement. HR should develop programs that prioritize employee well-being, mental health, and professional development. These programs could include counseling services, stress management workshops, and upskilling opportunities to help employees adapt to changing circumstances and feel valued by the organization.

4. Contingency Plans

Preparing for a range of scenarios is crucial for minimizing disruptions. HR should create contingency plans that address potential outcomes such as workforce reductions, budget cuts, or adjustments to operational procedures. These plans should outline specific actions to be taken in each scenario, ensuring that the organization can respond swiftly and strategically

5. Regular Review and Updates

A crisis management plan is not a static document. To remain effective, it must be regularly reviewed and updated to reflect evolving circumstances and incorporate lessons learned from previous crises. By keeping the plan current, HR ensures that the organization is always prepared to respond to emerging challenges with agility and confidence.

By developing and implementing these comprehensive crisis management plans, HR can play a pivotal role in guiding the organization through periods of economic uncertainty, safeguarding its long-term stability, and fostering a culture of resilience and adaptability.

Example: BP's Crisis Management Plan

In the wake of the Deepwater Horizon oil spill in 2010, BP faced a significant crisis that impacted its reputation, operations, and workforce. The company's HR team developed a comprehensive crisis management plan that included communication protocols, employee support initiatives, and ongoing training for managers on handling crisis situations. By proactively addressing the challenges posed by the crisis, BP was able to navigate the situation more effectively and focus on rebuilding trust with its stakeholders.

Leadership's Role in Crisis Management

Effective leadership is essential during economic downturns. HR must work closely with senior leaders to ensure that they are equipped to manage the challenges posed by a crisis. Leadership development programs that emphasize resilience, adaptability, and communication skills can help leaders navigate difficult situations and support their teams.

Case Study: Johnson & Johnson's Leadership During Crisis

During the Tylenol crisis in the 1980s, when cyanide-laced capsules led to consumer deaths, Johnson & Johnson's leadership demonstrated the importance of transparency and ethical decision-making. The CEO, James Burke, took immediate action to recall all Tylenol products and communicated openly with the public and employees about the steps being taken to address the crisis. HR played a key role in supporting leadership during this time, guiding communication strategies and employee engagement initiatives that focused on rebuilding trust.

Navigating economic downturns and managing crises demand a strategic and proactive approach from HR, as the success of an organization during challenging times heavily depends on the strength of its people and leadership. HR must take a comprehensive approach, beginning with clear and transparent communication. In times of uncertainty, employees look to leadership for direction and reassurance. Effective communication helps to reduce anxiety, build trust, and keep everyone aligned on the organization's goals and the steps needed to overcome challenges.

Employee support becomes even more crucial during a crisis. HR must provide resources to ensure the well-being of employees, from mental health initiatives to flexible work arrangements. Talent retention is another key area. During difficult times, retaining top talent becomes vital for future growth. HR should focus on identifying and nurturing high performers, offering them growth opportunities, and ensuring that they remain engaged and motivated, despite the external challenges.

Flexibility is also essential in crisis management. HR must adapt policies and practices to the changing environment, whether it's remote work, altered work hours, or shifts in benefits and compensation. Flexibility helps the workforce remain productive and engaged while accommodating the challenges of a crisis.

Moreover, leadership development plays a pivotal role in navigating tough times. HR must invest in developing strong, resilient leaders who can make critical decisions with confidence and guide their teams through uncertainty. These leaders not only steer their teams effectively but also inspire a sense of hope and perseverance in their employees.

In an increasingly unpredictable world, the role of HR in crisis management has never been more critical. By focusing on communication, employee support, talent retention, flexibility, and leadership development, HR ensures that organizations cannot only survive but thrive in adversity. HR acts as the anchor in turbulent waters, helping organizations emerge from crises stronger, more unified, and better prepared for future challenges.

"HR is the driving force in cultivating a green workforce, leading the charge for sustainability and forging a future where innovation and environmental responsibility go hand in hand."

CHAPTER 20

Sustainability and HR: Building a Green Workforce

– Cultivating a Greener Future

As the world increasingly confronts the impacts of climate change and environmental degradation, organizations are recognizing the importance of sustainability in their operations. Human Resources (HR) plays a critical role in this transformation by fostering a culture of sustainability, promoting eco-friendly practices, and engaging employees in initiatives that contribute to a greener future.

This chapter examines the role of HR in building a sustainable workforce, highlighting strategies, examples, and case studies that demonstrate how organizations can integrate sustainability into their HR practices.

Understanding Sustainability in the Workplace

Sustainability in the workplace involves creating an environment that meets present needs without compromising the ability of future generations to meet their own. This encompasses three key pillars: environmental stewardship, social responsibility, and economic viability. For HR, this means developing policies and practices that not only reduce the organization's environmental impact but also promote social equity and economic fairness.

Environmental Stewardship:

Organizations are adopting practices that minimize waste, reduce energy consumption, and lower carbon footprints. This can include initiatives like recycling programs, energy-efficient buildings, and sustainable sourcing practices.

Social Responsibility:

HR plays a role in ensuring that the organization operates ethically, treats employees fairly, and contributes positively to the communities in which it operates.

Economic Viability:

Sustainable practices can lead to cost savings, improved efficiency, and enhanced reputation, all of which contribute to the long-term success of the organization.

HR's Role in Promoting Sustainability

HR professionals are uniquely positioned to lead sustainability efforts within organizations. Here are several strategies HR can implement to cultivate a greener workforce:

1. Integrating Sustainability into Organizational Culture

Example: Unilever's Sustainable Living Plan

Unilever has long been recognized for its commitment to sustainability, exemplified through its Sustainable Living Plan, which aims to decouple growth from environmental impact. HR plays a vital role in embedding sustainability into the company's culture by incorporating sustainability goals into performance reviews, employee training, and leadership development programs.

The company's initiatives not only focus on reducing its carbon footprint but also engage employees at all levels to contribute ideas for sustainability. By fostering a culture of sustainability, Unilever has empowered employees to be part of the solution, resulting in innovative practices that drive the company's mission forward.

2. Sustainability Training and Development Programs

Example: Interface's Sustainability Learning

Interface, a global flooring manufacturer, has made significant strides in sustainability through its "Mission Zero" initiative, which aims to eliminate the company's negative environmental impact by 2020. To achieve this goal, HR has developed comprehensive training programs that educate employees about sustainability practices, including waste reduction, recycling, and energy efficiency.

Employees participate in workshops that teach them how to implement sustainable practices in their daily work. For example, Interface encourages employees to track their energy consumption and come up with innovative solutions to reduce waste. This commitment to sustainability not only enhances employee engagement but also drives significant operational improvements.

3. Green Employee Engagement Initiatives

Case Study: Google's Green Initiatives

Google has implemented numerous green initiatives aimed at engaging employees in sustainability efforts. The company's HR team promotes a culture of sustainability through programs such as "Green Teams," which are employee-led groups focused on promoting sustainable practices within their departments.

Google encourages employees to participate in sustainability challenges, such as reducing energy usage in the office, participating in local environmental clean-up events, and developing innovative ideas for making the workplace more eco-friendly. By fostering grassroots engagement, Google empowers employees to take ownership of sustainability efforts, resulting in a more environmentally conscious workforce.

Implementing Sustainable HR Practices

To support sustainability initiatives, HR professionals should consider the following practices:

1. Sustainable Recruitment and Selection

Example: Patagonia's Hiring Practices

Outdoor clothing retailer Patagonia integrates sustainability into its recruitment process by seeking candidates who share the company's commitment to environmental responsibility. The HR team assesses candidates not only on their skills and experience ,but also on their passion for sustainability and adherence to ethical practices.

By hiring individuals who align with its values, Patagonia reinforces its mission to protect the environment and encourages a culture of sustainability throughout the organization.

2. Green Workplace Policies

Example: Salesforce's Green Building Standards

Salesforce, a global leader in cloud computing, has made sustainability a core component of its workplace design.

The company adheres to green building standards, ensuring that its offices are designed to minimize environmental impact through energy-efficient lighting, sustainable materials, and waste reduction practices.

HR plays a critical role in promoting these policies, educating employees about their benefits, and encouraging them to embrace eco-friendly behaviors in the workplace.

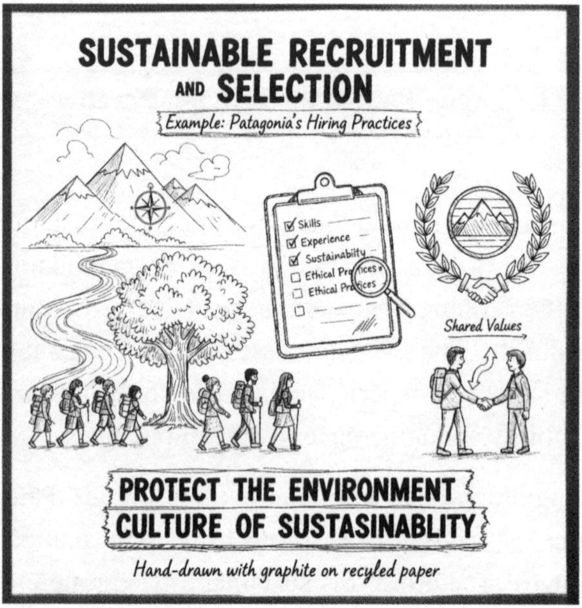

3. Measuring and Reporting Sustainability Effort

Case Study: IKEA's Sustainability Reporting

IKEA has established a comprehensive sustainability framework that includes setting clear goals, measuring progress, and publicly reporting on its sustainability initiatives. HR is integral to this process, as it collects data on employee engagement in sustainability programs, tracks the success of green initiatives, and reports findings to stakeholders.

By maintaining transparency about its sustainability efforts, IKEA builds trust with both employees and customers, while demonstrating its commitment to being a responsible corporate citizen.

Challenges in Implementing Sustainability Initiatives

While integrating sustainability into HR practices presents significant opportunities for organizations to align with global goals and enhance their reputation, it also comes with a unique set of challenges. These challenges must be addressed thoughtfully to ensure the successful adoption and long-term impact of sustainability initiatives. The key challenges include:

1. **Resistance to Change**

   Resistance to change is one of the most common barriers to implementing sustainability initiatives. Employees may be hesitant to embrace new practices, especially if they perceive these changes as additional workloads, disruptions, or unnecessary inconveniences. For instance, adopting sustainable work practices like reducing paper use or altering long-standing workflows may encounter pushback from employees who are comfortable with the status quo. Overcoming this resistance requires effective communication, education, and the involvement of employees in the planning and implementation process to foster a sense of ownership and commitment.

2. **Resource Constraints**

   Many sustainability initiatives require significant upfront investments in areas such as training, technology, and infrastructure. For example, transitioning to energy-efficient systems, implementing recycling programs, or providing sustainability-focused employee training can strain financial and operational resources, particularly for small-to-mid-sized organizations. Balancing these initial costs with the long-term benefits of sustainability can be challenging, especially in organizations with tight budgets or competing priorities. HR must collaborate with leadership to prioritize initiatives that deliver the highest impact while being mindful of resource limitations.

3. **Measuring Impact**

   Quantifying the outcomes of sustainability initiatives can be complex, particularly when the benefits are long-term or intangible. For example, reducing carbon emissions or improving employee well-being through sustainability programs may not yield immediate, measurable returns. This lack of clear metrics makes it difficult to calculate ROI and may hinder efforts to secure ongoing support from leadership and stakeholders. HR must develop robust measurement frameworks that incorporate both qualitative and quantitative data to effectively communicate the value and progress of sustainability efforts.

By acknowledging and proactively addressing these challenges, organizations can create a strong foundation for the successful integration of sustainability into HR practices. This includes fostering a culture of openness and collaboration, securing adequate resources, and leveraging innovative tools and strategies to track and showcase the tangible and intangible benefits of sustainability initiatives. Through these efforts, organizations can ensure that sustainability becomes a core component of their HR strategy, driving long-term value for employees, the business, and the broader community.

As organizations increasingly recognize the importance of sustainability, HR professionals must play a proactive and central role in driving these initiatives. It begins with effectively communicating the long-term benefits of sustainability to employees at all levels. HR can highlight how sustainable practices not only help the environment but also contribute to the organization's long-term success and the well-being of its workforce. By clearly articulating these benefits, HR can foster a deeper understanding and commitment to sustainability throughout the organization.

In addition to communication, HR must provide the necessary resources and support to ensure sustainability goals are achievable. This includes offering training programs that educate employees on environmentally friendly practices, providing tools and technologies that facilitate sustainable work practices, and creating opportunities for employees to engage in sustainability efforts, both inside and outside the workplace. HR can also ensure that sustainability is woven into company policies, from energy-efficient office practices to promoting remote work options that reduce carbon footprints.

Another crucial aspect is developing clear metrics to track the organization's progress towards its sustainability goals. HR can work with other departments to establish key performance indicators (KPIs) that measure the success of sustainability initiatives, such as reductions in energy usage, waste, and carbon emissions. Regularly evaluating these metrics ensures that the company remains accountable and can make data-driven adjustments to its strategies as needed.

Furthermore, HR can integrate sustainability into recruitment and retention strategies. By seeking out candidates who share the organization's commitment to environmental responsibility, HR helps build a workforce that is aligned with the company's sustainability mission. Training programs can then reinforce this commitment, encouraging employees to contribute to sustainability both in their professional and personal lives.

Ultimately, as sustainability becomes a global priority, HR professionals are not just responsible for managing human resources—they are also integral in shaping the company's environmental impact. By embedding sustainability into recruitment practices, employee development, and workplace policies, HR can help organizations achieve their sustainability goals while fostering a culture of environmental responsibility. As the demand for green initiatives continues to rise, HR will be at the forefront of this transformative movement, driving change and cultivating a greener future that benefits both organizations and society as a whole.

"The future of HR lies in its ability to innovate and adapt, transforming tomorrow's workforce with bold insights, disruptive strategies, and relentless forward-thinking."

CHAPTER 21

The Future of HR - Emerging Trends and Predictions :

Shaping Tomorrow's Workforce with Innovation and Insights

As the global workforce continues to evolve, so too does the role of Human Resources. HR professionals are at the forefront of navigating emerging trends and leveraging innovative technologies to shape the future of work. From the impact of artificial intelligence and automation to shifting employee expectations and the rise of the gig economy, HR is transforming to meet the demands of a rapidly changing world.

The landscape of human resources is rapidly evolving as technology, societal changes, and shifting workforce dynamics redefine the future of work. As organizations strive to remain competitive in a fast-paced global market, HR professionals must anticipate emerging trends and leverage innovation to shape tomorrow's workforce.

This chapter examines the key drivers of change in HR, with a focus on the impact of AI and automation, the evolving employer-employee relationship, and how HR can prepare for the next generation of global workers. It also explores the key trends shaping the future of HR and how organizations can prepare to stay ahead in a competitive global market.

The Impact of AI and Automation on the Global Workforce

Artificial intelligence (AI) and automation are revolutionizing how organizations operate and manage their workforce. AI-powered tools are enabling HR teams to streamline recruitment processes, enhance employee engagement, and improve decision-making. However, the rise of automation also raises concerns about job displacement and the need for employees to reskill and upskill in order to remain competitive in an increasingly automated world.

Example: AI-Driven Recruitment at a Global E-Commerce Company

A leading global e-commerce company implemented an AI-driven recruitment platform to manage the influx of job applications it received for various positions. The platform used machine learning algorithms to analyze resumes, screen candidates, and predict which applicants were most likely to succeed in the company. By automating the initial stages of the recruitment process, the HR team was able to focus on interviewing and evaluating top candidates, reducing the time-to-hire by 30%.

Additionally, the AI platform helped eliminate unconscious bias in the recruitment process by using objective data to assess candidates' qualifications. This led to a more diverse and inclusive workforce, as the system prioritized skills and experience over subjective factors. The company's HR team also used AI-powered chatbots to provide real-time updates to candidates, improving the candidate experience and increasing engagement.

While these technologies bring new opportunities, they also present challenges that HR leaders must address proactively.

1. Redefining Job Roles and Skill Sets

AI and automation are automating repetitive and low-skill tasks, leading to the emergence of more complex and strategic roles that require advanced problem-solving, creativity, and emotional intelligence. HR professionals must anticipate these changes and identify which roles may become obsolete or transformed. Organizations should focus on upskilling and reskilling their employees, ensuring that they are equipped with the skills necessary to thrive in an AI-driven world.

2. Augmenting Human Capabilities

Rather than replacing human workers, AI can augment their capabilities by automating routine tasks, providing data-driven insights, and supporting decision-making processes. For instance, AI-powered tools can streamline the recruitment process by screening resumes, predicting candidate success, and enhancing the overall hiring experience. In this context, HR must foster a culture where humans and AI collaborate effectively, leveraging technology to enhance human potential.

3. Managing Workforce Displacement

As AI and automation reshape industries, workforce displacement is inevitable. HR will play a critical role in managing the transition by providing career development programs, offering support for displaced workers, and facilitating smooth transitions into new roles. By prioritizing employee well-being and continuous learning, HR can ensure that the workforce remains adaptable and resilient in the face of technological disruption.

The Evolving Nature of the Employer-Employee Relationship

The traditional employer-employee relationship is changing as workers increasingly seek flexibility, purpose, and autonomy in their careers. Today's employees, particularly millennials and Gen Z, prioritize work-life balance, personal development, and alignment with company values. In response, organizations are shifting their focus from managing employees to creating environments that foster collaboration, engagement, and personal fulfillment.

1. From Employment to Partnership

Historically, the employer-employee relationship was characterized by a hierarchical structure, with the employer dictating terms and the employee adhering to them. However, this dynamic shifts as employees increasingly seek autonomy, flexibility, and meaning in their work. The relationship is evolving into a partnership, where both parties work together to achieve mutual goals. HR must foster this new dynamic by creating policies that encourage open communication, empower employees, and align individual aspirations with organizational objectives.

2. The Rise of the Gig Economy and Flexible Work

The gig economy, characterized by freelance, contract, and short-term work, is growing globally. Additionally, flexible work arrangements such as remote work and part-time employment are becoming more prevalent. HR leaders must adapt to this trend by developing policies that support non-traditional work models while ensuring compliance with labour laws, fair compensation, and benefits. Creating a flexible and inclusive work environment will be key to attracting and retaining top talent.

3. Employee Experience and Engagement

In the future, employee experience will be a top priority for HR, as organizations recognize that engaged employees are more productive, innovative, and loyal. HR must focus on creating personalized employee experiences that cater to diverse needs, such as mental health support, career development opportunities, and work-life balance initiatives. Investing in employee well-being and creating a sense of purpose at work will be essential for building a committed and engaged workforce.

Example: Flexible Work Arrangements in a Global Consulting Firm

A global consulting firm recognized that its employees were seeking greater flexibility in how and where they worked. To accommodate this, the company implemented a flexible work policy that allowed employees to choose between working remotely, in the office, or a hybrid model. The policy also gave employees the freedom to set their own work hours, as long as they met project deadlines.

This shift not only improved employee satisfaction and retention but also boosted productivity. Employees appreciated the ability to balance work with personal commitments, leading to a more engaged and motivated workforce. HR also played a key role in ensuring that remote employees felt connected to the company culture by organizing virtual team-building activities and maintaining regular communication.

Preparing for the Next Generation of Global Workers

As Gen Z enters the workforce and millennials move into leadership positions, the expectations and behaviors of the global workforce are shifting. HR professionals must be attuned to the unique needs of these generations and prepare for the future by embracing forward-thinking strategies.

1. Emphasizing Purpose-Driven Work

Younger generations place a high value on purpose-driven work that aligns with their values and contributes to societal good. HR leaders should promote corporate social responsibility (CSR) initiatives, sustainability efforts, and ethical business practices to attract and retain talent. By fostering a sense of purpose, organizations can engage employees who are motivated by making a positive impact on the world.

2. Championing Diversity and Inclusion

The next generation of workers is highly diverse in terms of race, gender, sexual orientation, and socio-economic backgrounds. They expect employers to prioritize diversity and inclusion, not just as a compliance issue but as a core value. HR must implement initiatives that create an inclusive culture where everyone feels valued and has equal opportunities for growth. This includes addressing unconscious bias in recruitment, providing mentorship programs, and promoting diverse leadership.

3. Leveraging Technology for Workforce Development

Digital natives expect technology to be an integral part of their work experience. HR must embrace digital tools for learning, development, and career progression.

This includes using AI for personalized learning paths, gamifying training programs, and offering virtual reality (VR) simulations for skill development. By leveraging technology, HR can create engaging and future-focused learning environments that prepare the workforce for ongoing innovation.

Example: Gig Economy Integration at a Multinational Corporation

A multinational corporation facing project-based demands decided to integrate gig workers into its workforce to increase agility and tap into specialized skills. The HR team developed a platform that enabled the company to manage both gig workers and full-time employees, ensuring seamless collaboration between two groups. The platform included features for onboarding, managing project timelines, and compensating gig workers based on their contributions.

By embracing the gig economy, the company gained access to a global pool of skilled workers who could be hired on demand to meet project needs. This model provided the flexibility to scale the workforce up or down based on business demands, without the long-term commitments associated with traditional employment contracts. HR played a crucial role in ensuring that gig workers felt integrated into the company's culture and had access to the resources they needed to succeed.

Embracing Diversity, Equity, and Inclusion (DEI)

As the global workforce becomes more diverse, organizations are placing greater emphasis on diversity, equity, and inclusion (DEI) initiatives. HR professionals are tasked with creating inclusive work environments that celebrate diversity and promote equal opportunities for all employees. DEI is no longer just a compliance requirement; it is a strategic priority that drives innovation, employee engagement, and business success.

Example: DEI Programs in a Global Tech Company

A global tech company recognized the need to improve diversity and inclusion within its workforce, particularly in leadership roles. The HR team launched a series of DEI programs that included mentorship and leadership development opportunities for underrepresented groups, unconscious bias training for all employees, and partnerships with diverse organizations to expand its talent pipeline.

In addition to improving representation, the company introduced policies that promote equity, including pay transparency and inclusive benefits packages. These efforts resulted in a more diverse leadership team and improved employee satisfaction, as employees felt valued and supported in their career development. HR's focus on DEI also contributed to the company's reputation as an inclusive and innovative workplace, helping to attract top talent from diverse backgrounds.

The Rise of Data-Driven HR Decision Making

Data analytics is transforming HR by providing valuable insights into employee behavior, performance, and engagement. HR teams are increasingly using data to make informed decisions about talent management, workforce planning, and employee development. Predictive analytics, in particular, is helping HR professionals anticipate workforce trends, identify potential challenges, and implement proactive solutions.

Example: Predictive Analytics in Talent Management

A global financial services firm implemented a data-driven approach to talent management by using predictive analytics to identify high-potential employees and anticipate turnover risks. The HR team analyzed employee performance data, engagement surveys, and career progression trends to predict which employees were most likely to succeed in leadership roles.

The insights gained from predictive analytics enabled HR to develop targeted development programs for high-potential employees, ensuring they received the necessary training and support to advance within the company.

Additionally, the data helped HR identify potential retention risks and implement personalized retention strategies, such as offering flexible work arrangements or career development opportunities. By leveraging data-driven decision-making, the company was able to improve talent retention and succession planning.

The Future of Employee Well-Being

Employee well-being is becoming a central focus of HR, as organizations recognize the link between well-being and productivity. In the future, HR will take a more holistic approach to employee well-being, encompassing not only physical health but also mental and emotional wellness. Companies that prioritize employee well-being are more likely to attract and retain top talent, as well-being becomes a key consideration for workers when choosing an employer.

Example: Mental Health Initiatives in a Global Law Firm

A global law firm launched a mental health and well-being initiative after recognizing the high levels of stress and burnout among its employees. The HR team introduced wellness programs that included access to mental health professionals, stress management workshops, and flexible work options to reduce burnout.

HR also implemented policies that encouraged employees to take regular breaks, use their vacation time, and disconnect from work outside of business hours. These initiatives significantly improved employee well-being and reduced stress-related turnover. By prioritizing mental health, the firm created a healthier and more sustainable work environment, contributing to higher employee satisfaction and retention.

The future of HR is being shaped by a confluence of technological advancements, evolving workforce expectations, and the growing need for flexible, inclusive, and data-driven strategies in managing talent. As AI and automation continue to impact industries, HR professionals must take the lead in equipping employees with the skills necessary to thrive in this new landscape. This involves upskilling and reskilling initiatives, managing workforce transitions, and ensuring a smooth collaboration between human expertise and emerging technologies. Moreover, as the nature of work shifts, the traditional employer-employee relationship is evolving into a more flexible and collaborative partnership. HR must adapt to these changes by embracing new work models, promoting employee experience, and ensuring that the organization remains adaptable to future trends.

Equally important is HR's role in fostering diversity, equity, and inclusion in the workplace, which has become a central expectation for the next generation of workers.

As organizations prepare for a more inclusive and purpose-driven workforce, HR must create environments that not only meet the demands of technological advancement but also prioritize employee well-being. By incorporating data-driven decision-making, HR can fine-tune policies and processes that improve organizational efficiency, while fostering a culture of transparency and continuous learning. By staying ahead of these emerging trends—such as AI, flexible work models, diversity, and well-being—HR professionals can develop forward-thinking strategies that empower employees, drive business success, and position organizations to thrive in a rapidly evolving world.